My learning goals and success criteria:

- *I can trace and write all lower-case letters of the alphabet.*
- *I can trace and write all capital letters of the alphabet.*
- *I can trace and write the numerals 1 to 10.*

Are you ready to write?

Posture

Is your back resting against the chair?

Are your feet flat on the floor?

Paper position

left-handed

Are you holding the paper steady with your non-writing hand?

right-handed

Pencil grip

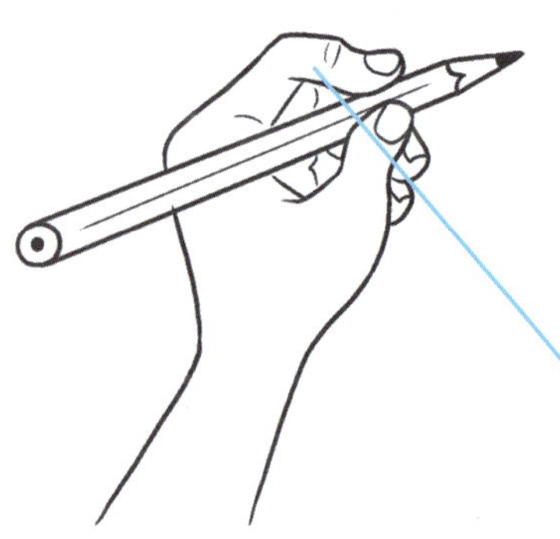

Is one finger on top of the pencil?

Left-handers, hold your pencil a little further up so you can see your handwriting!

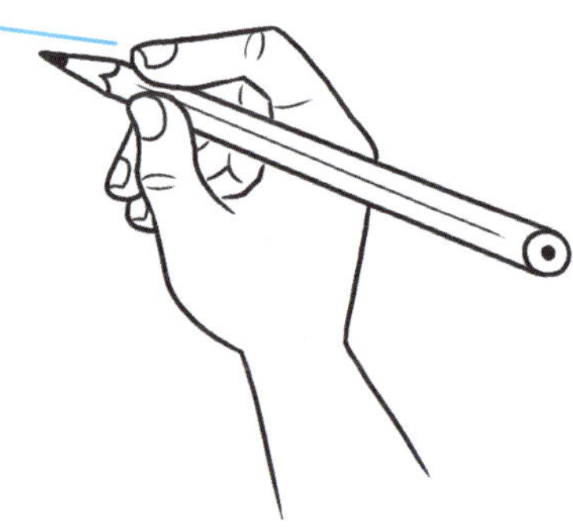

1, 2, 3, 4! Are my feet flat on the floor?
5, 6, 7, 8! Is my back up nice and straight?
9, 10, 11, 12! Show me how your pencil's held!
Thumb and pointer side-by-side, lucky tall one takes a ride!

Start at the blue dots. Follow the arrows.

Start at the blue dots. Follow the arrows.

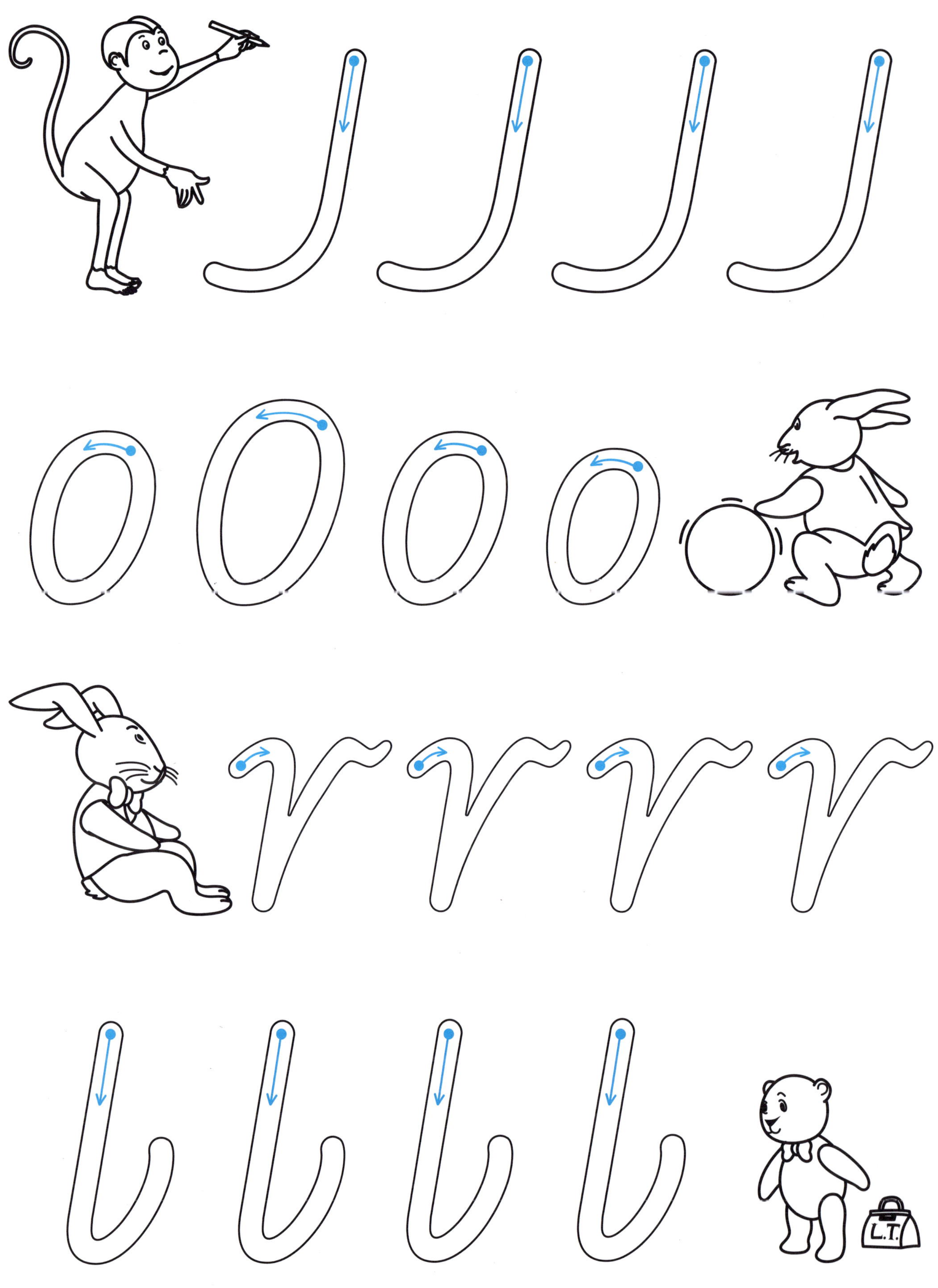

Start at the blue dots. Follow the arrows.

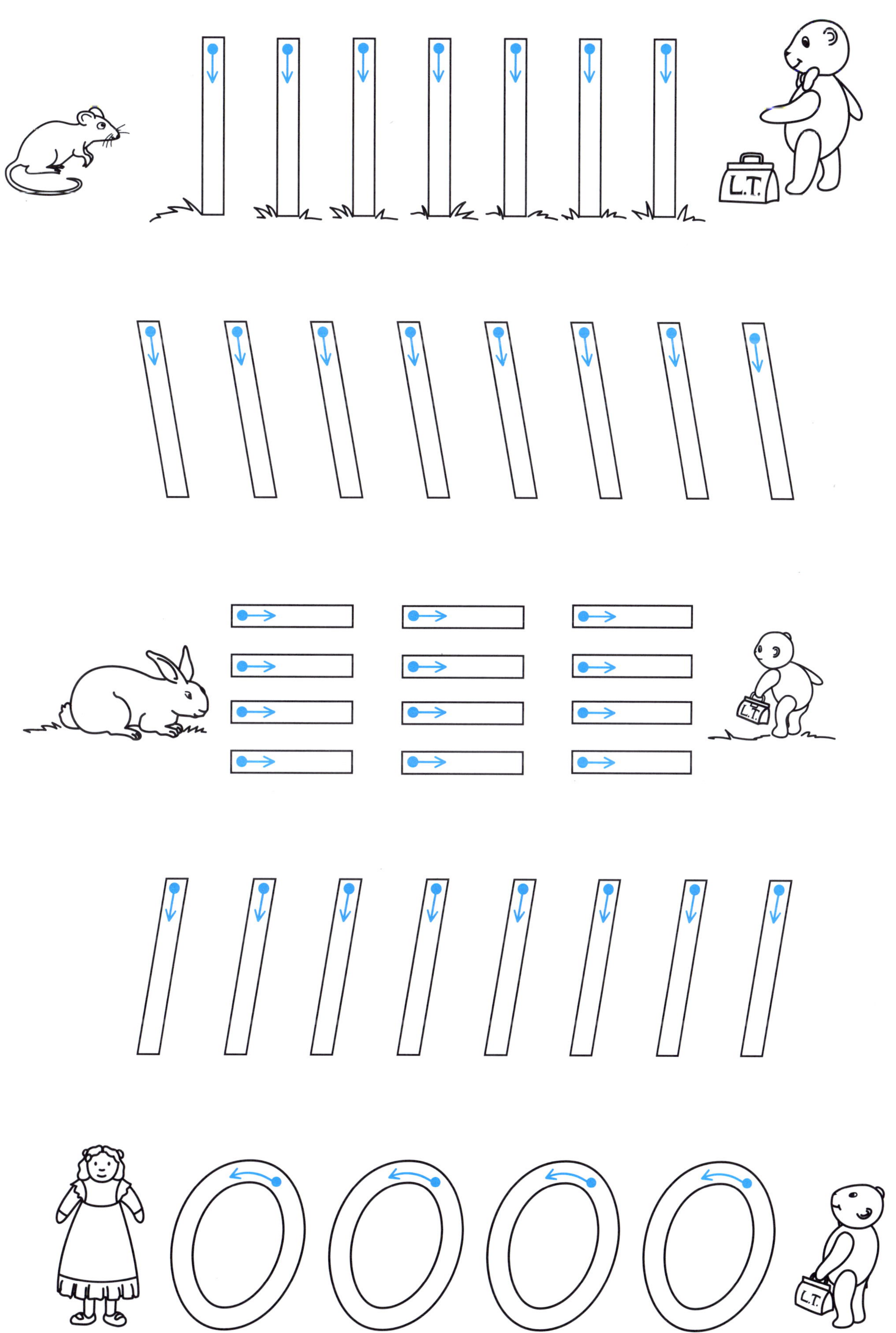

Start at the blue dots. Follow the arrows.

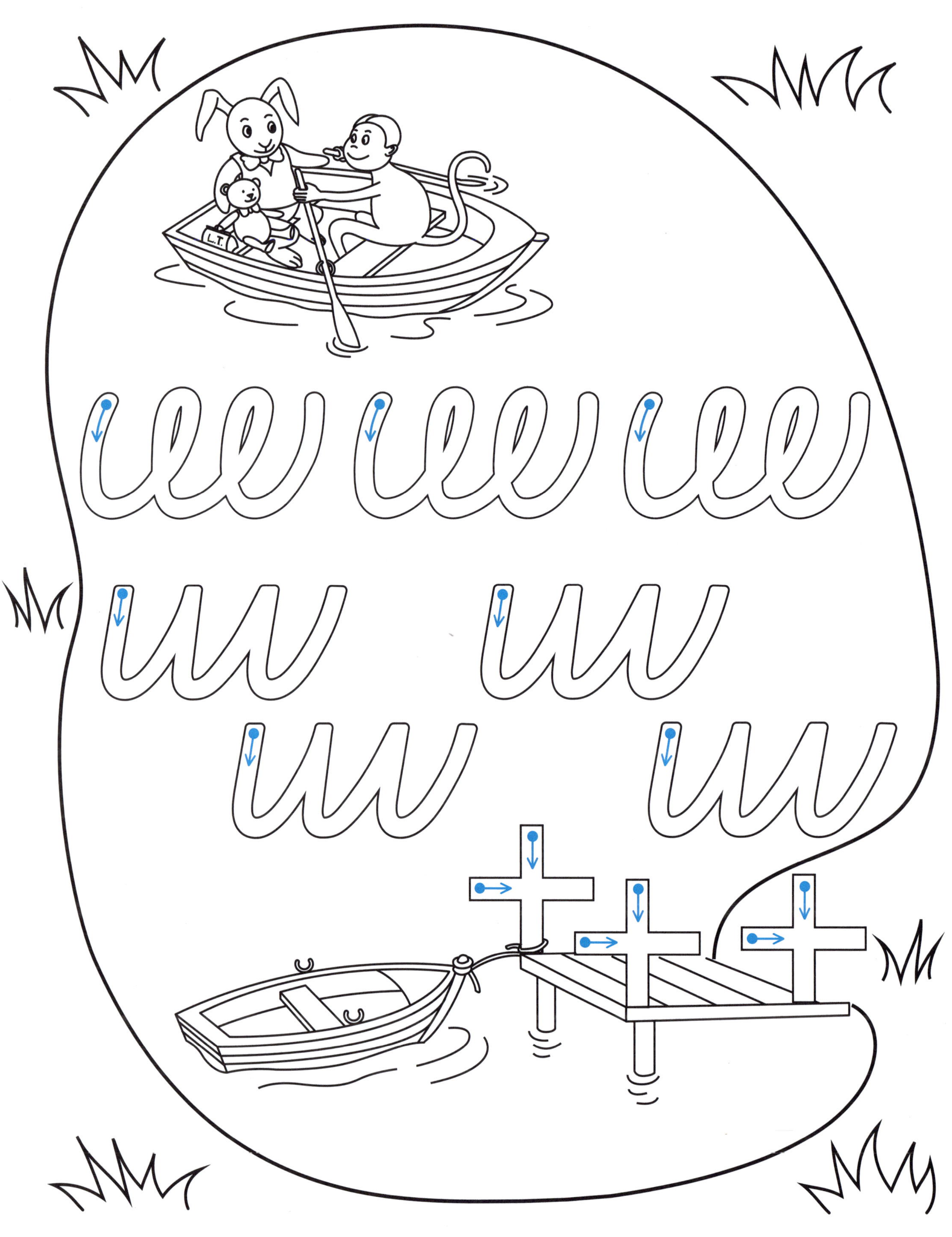

Start at the blue dots. Follow the arrows.

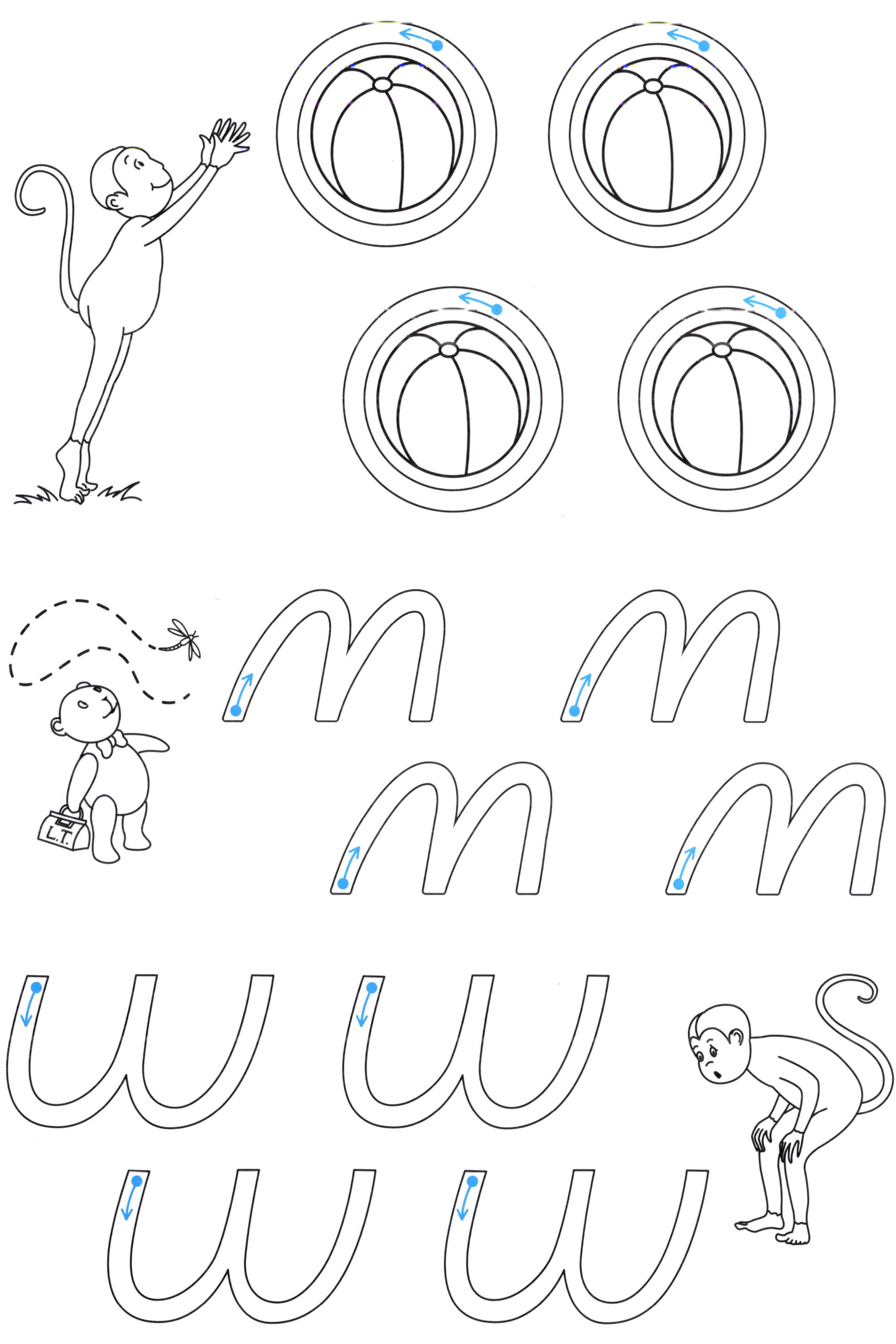

Start at the blue dots. Follow the arrows.

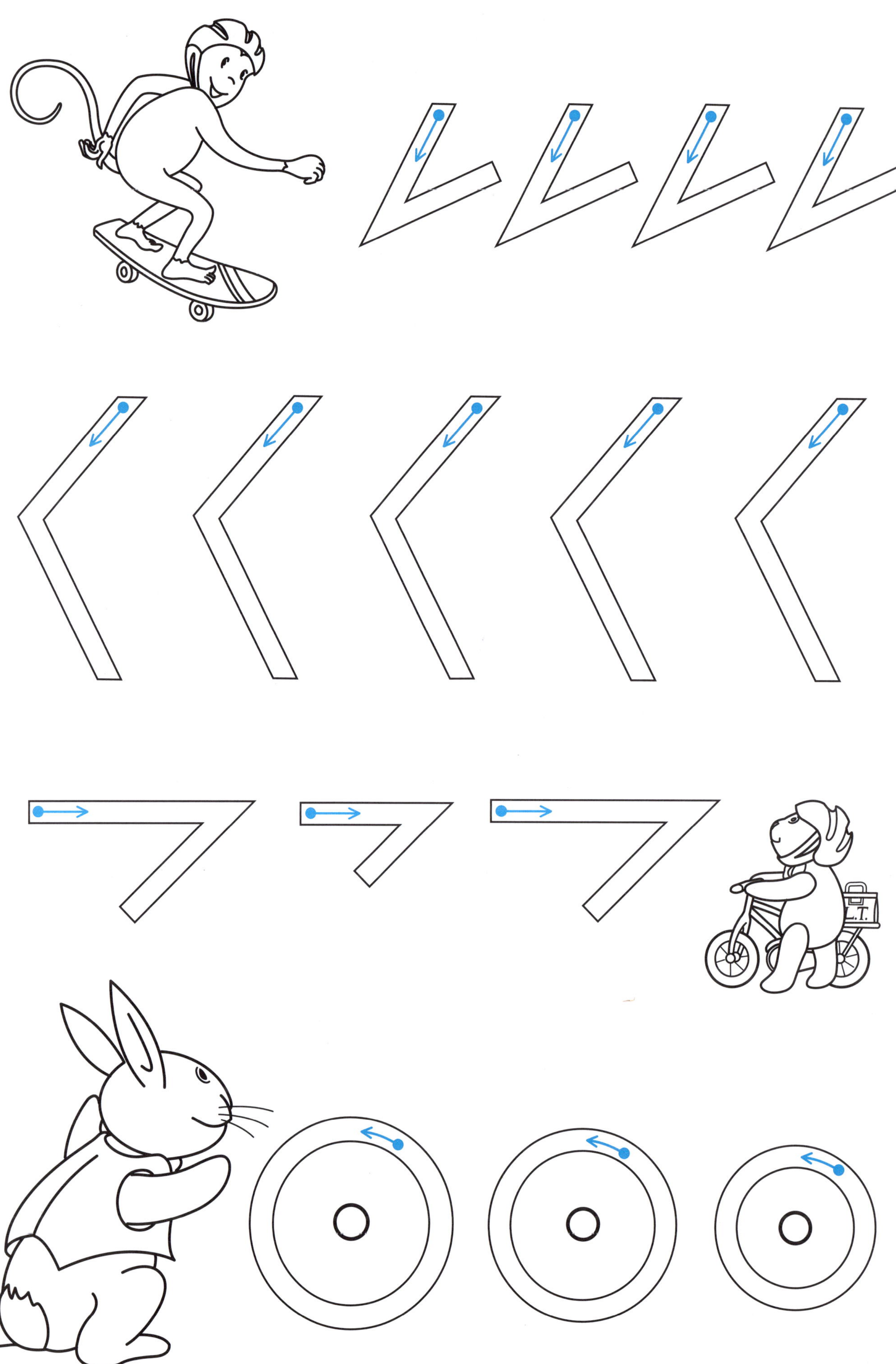

Start at the blue dots. Follow the arrows.

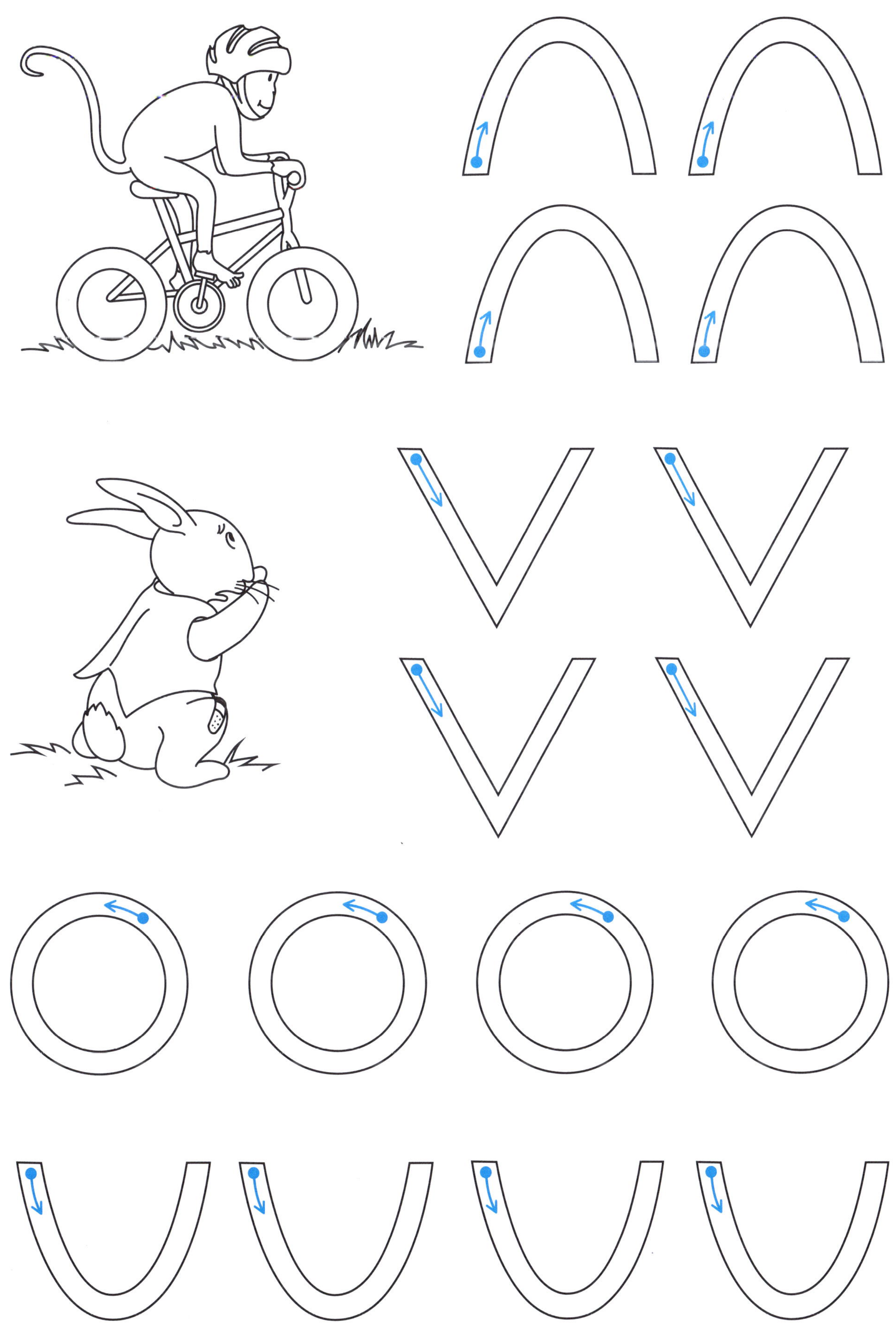

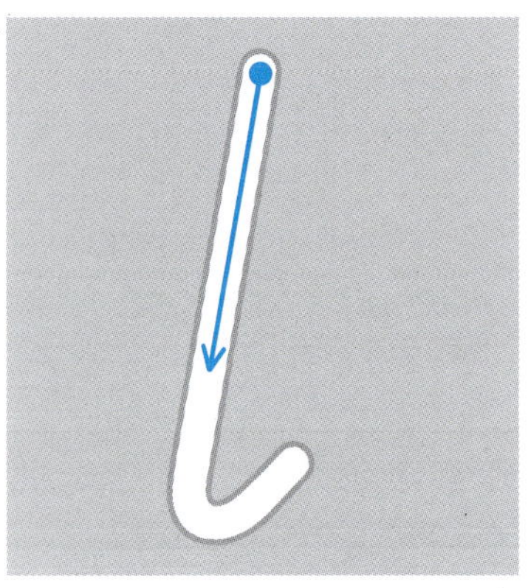

ladder

Start at the dot. Follow the arrow.

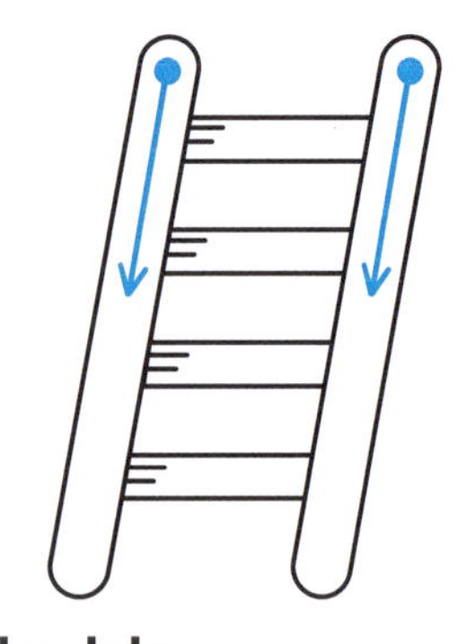

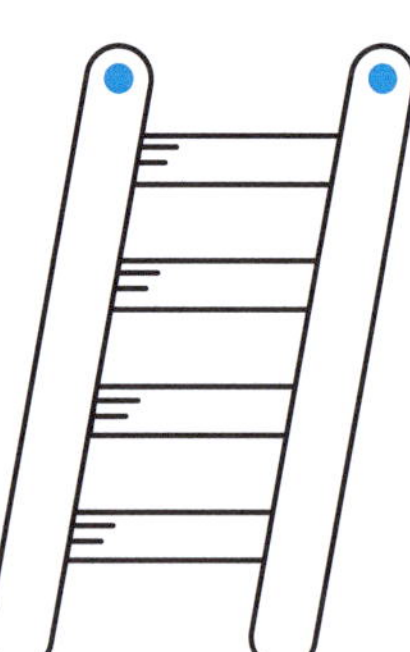

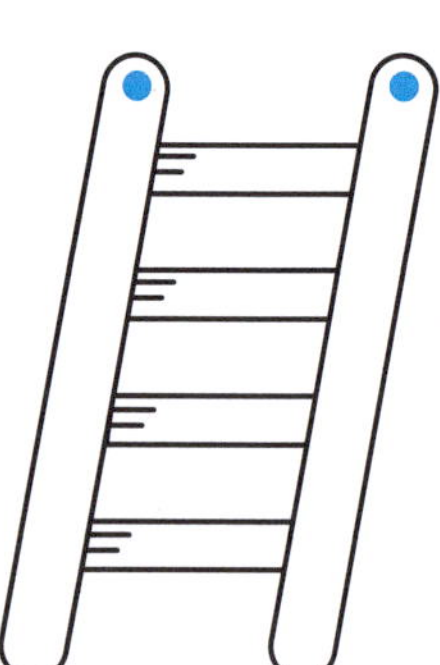

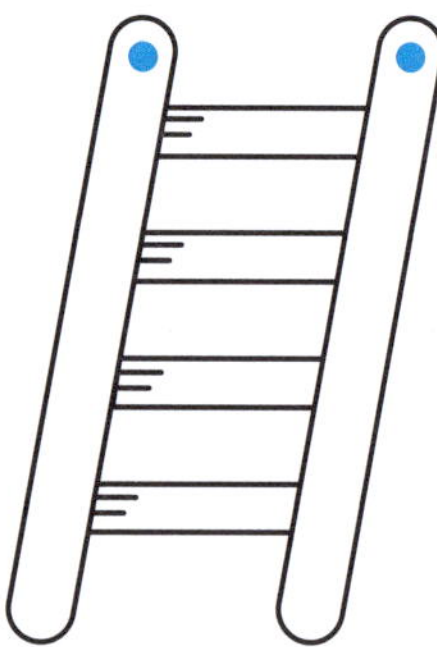

ladder

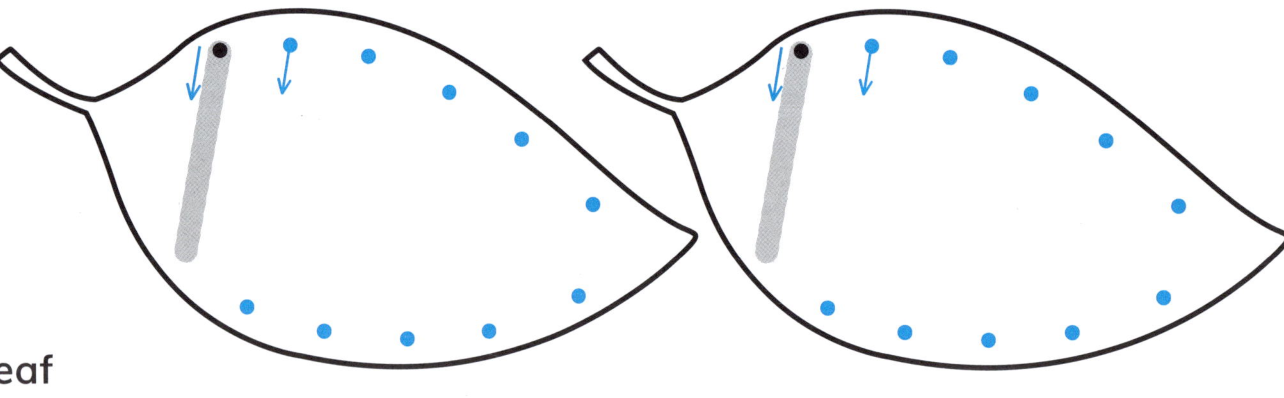

leaf

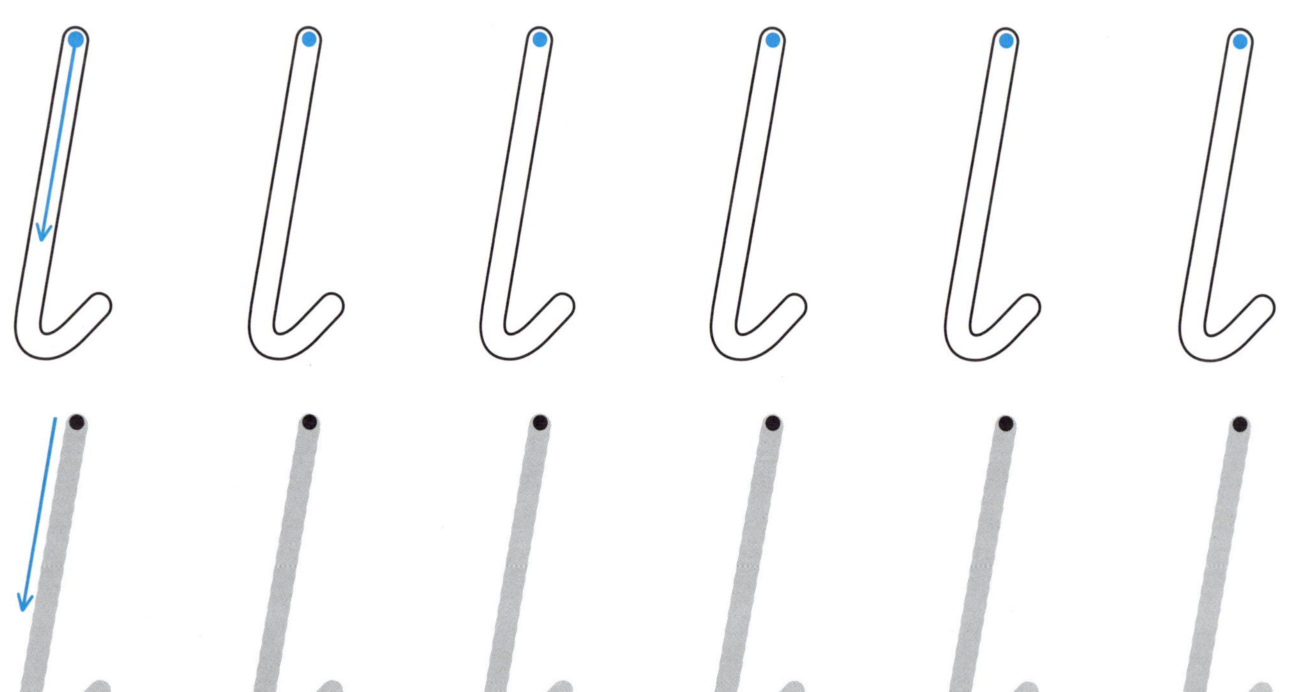

leopard

Trace the letter.

look look look

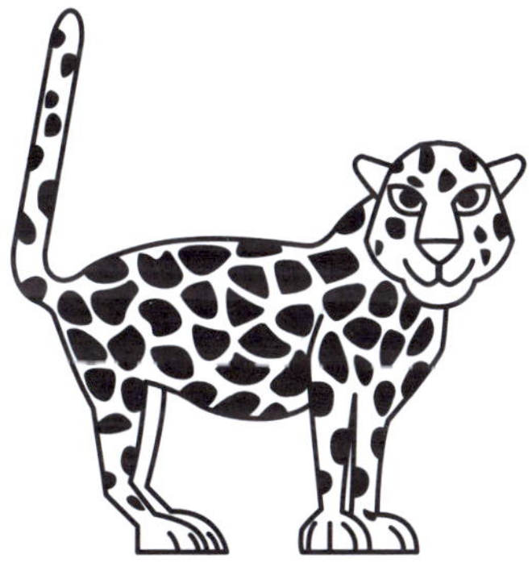

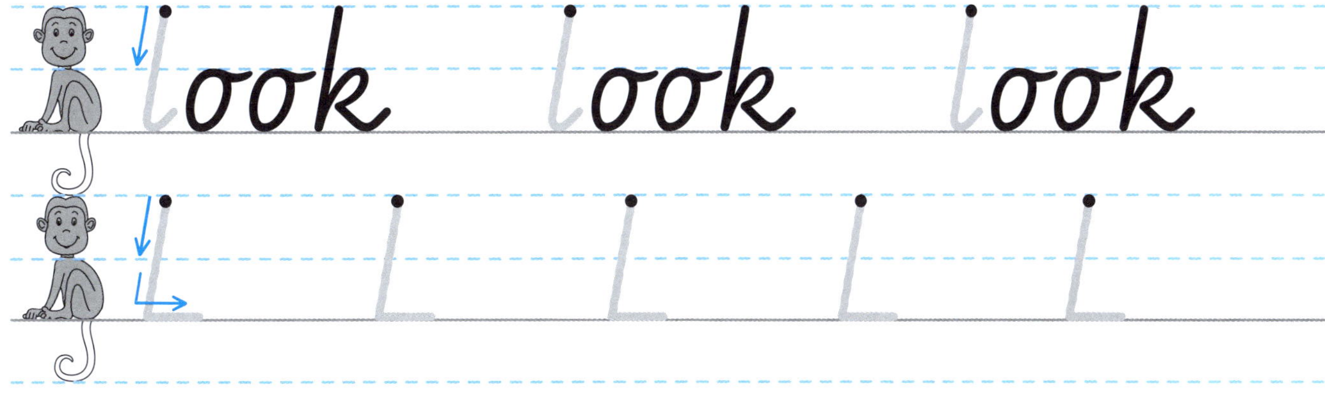

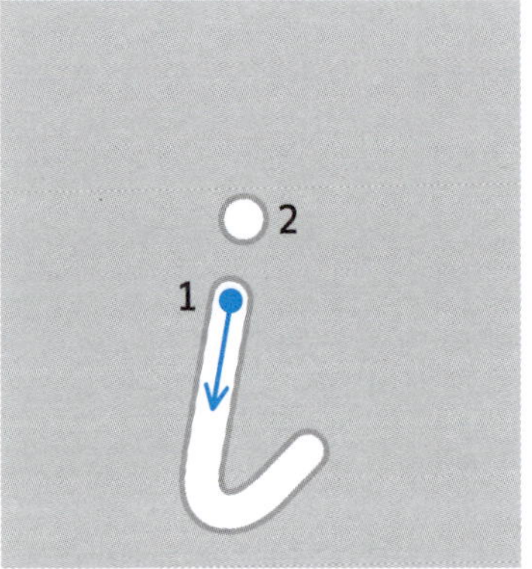

insects

Start at the dot. Follow the arrow.

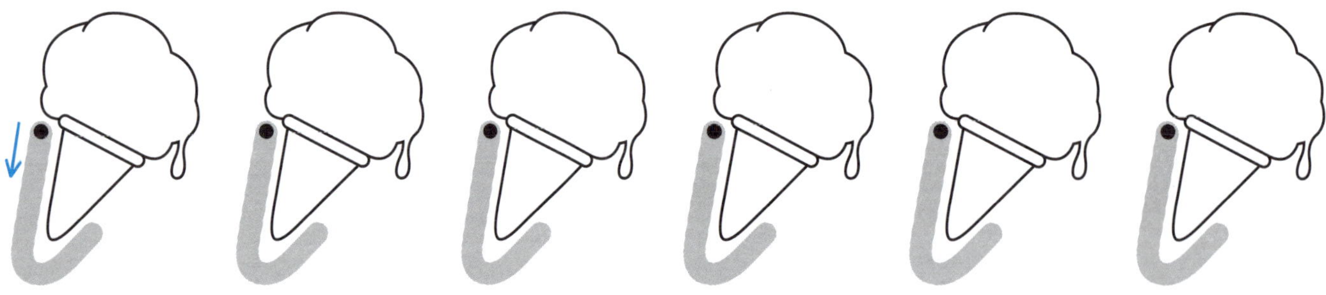

ice cream

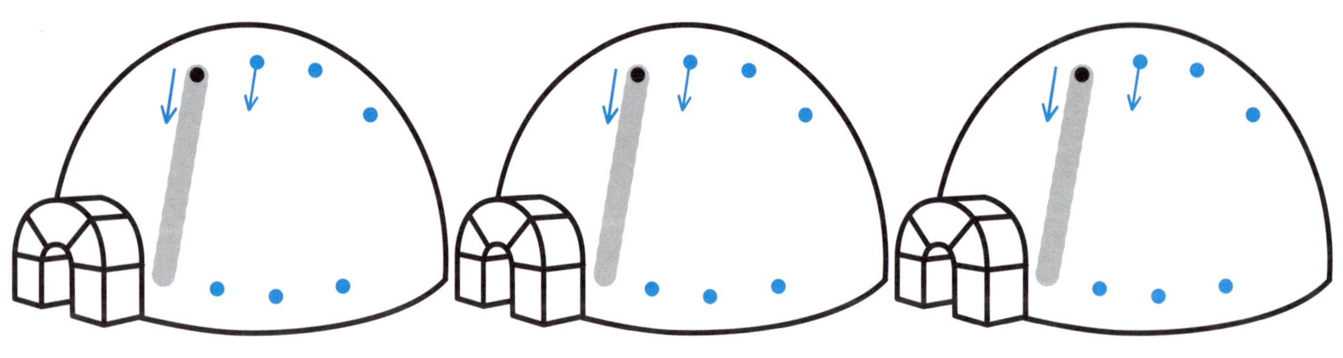

igloo

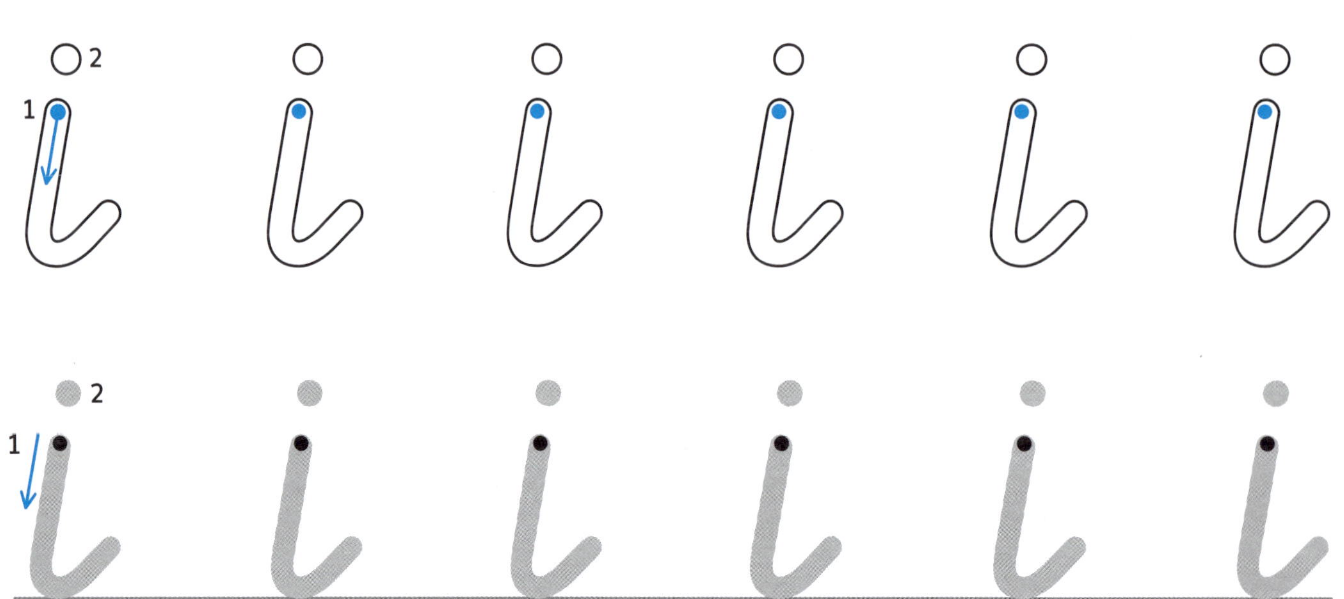

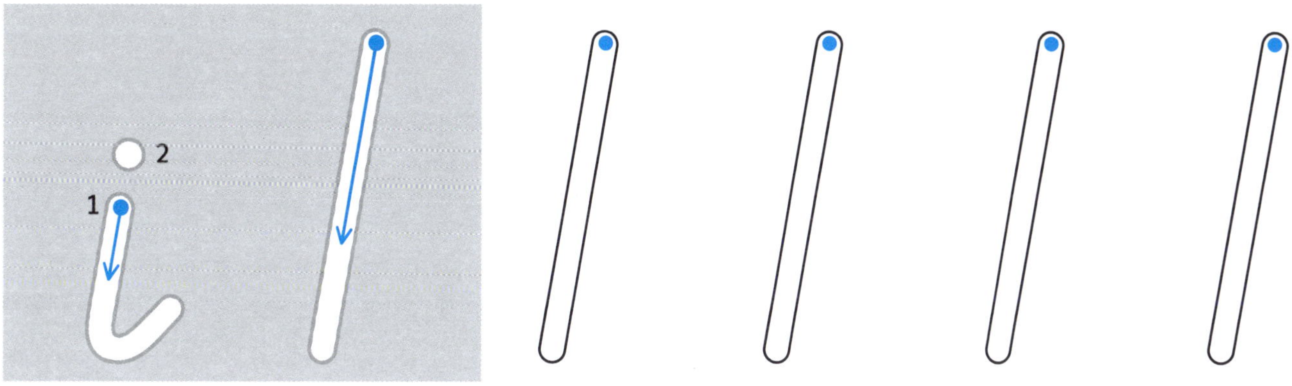

1 2

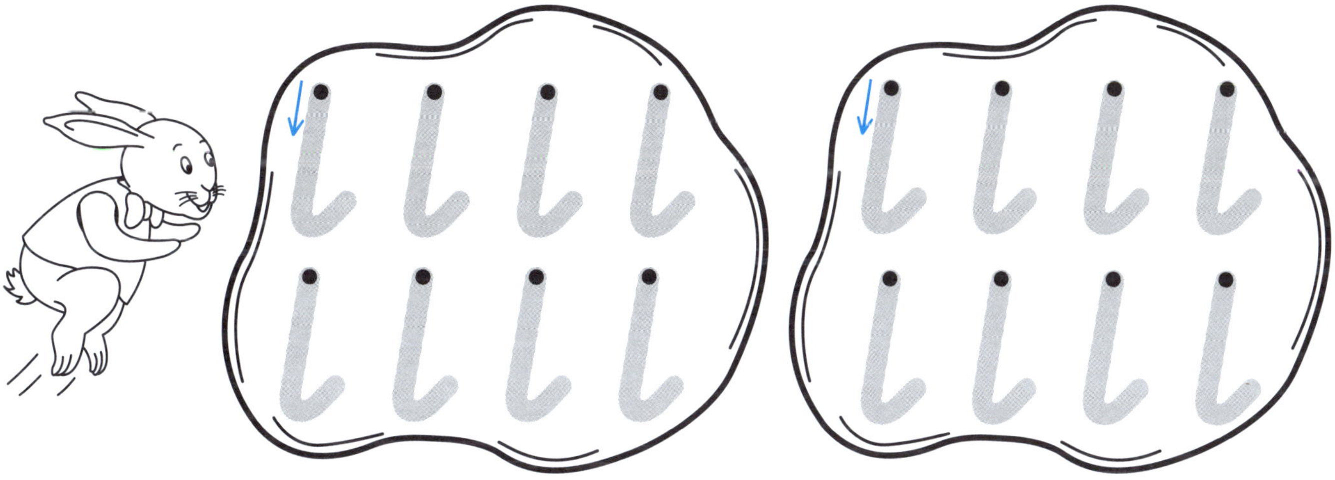

jump in

island

Trace the letter.

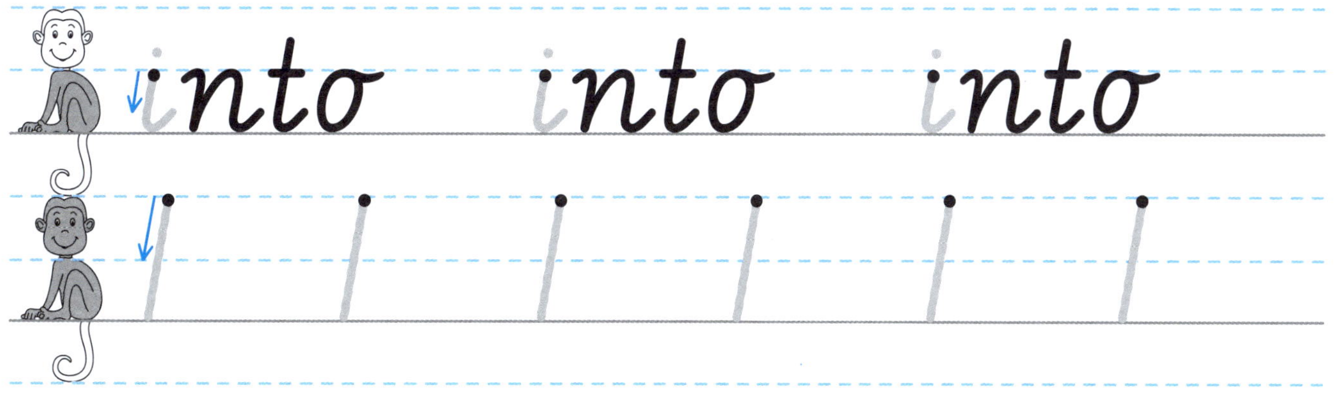

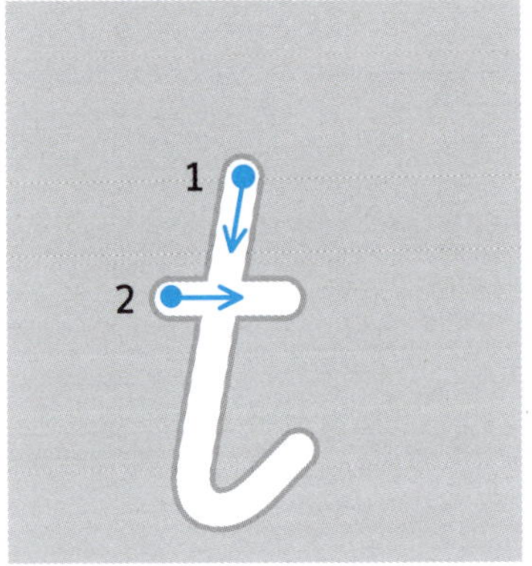

tree

Start at the dot. Follow the arrow.

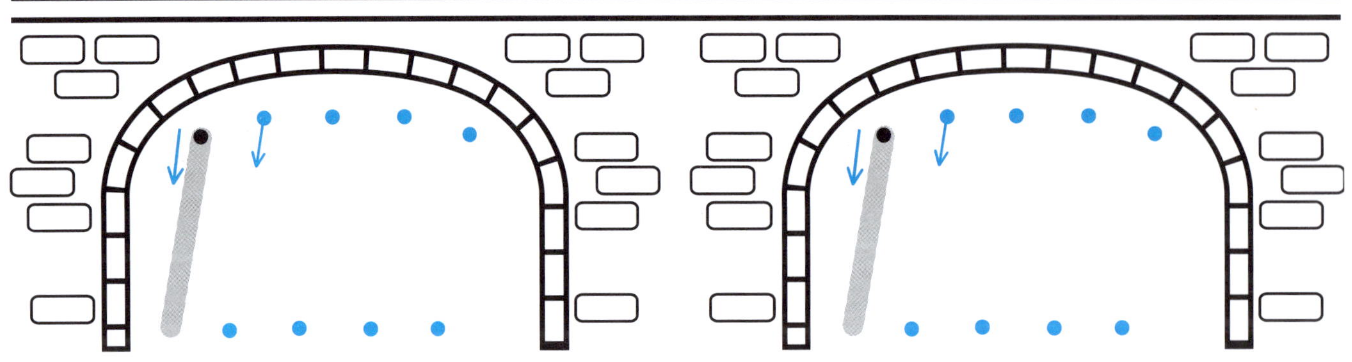

tunnels

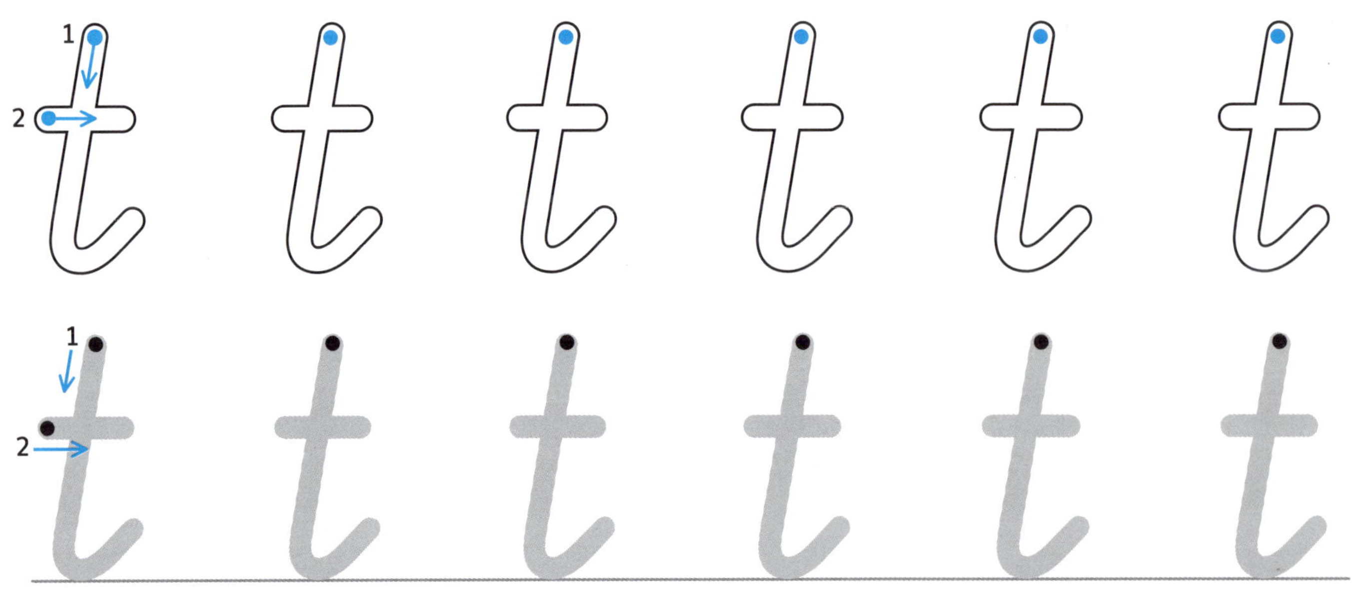

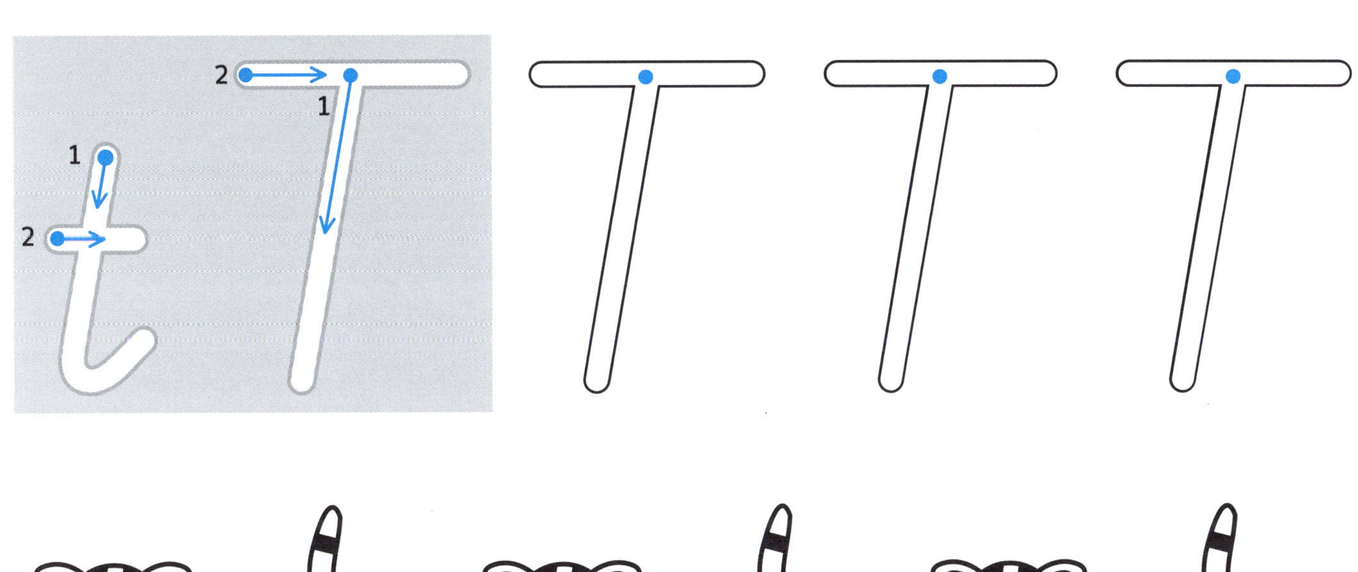

tiger

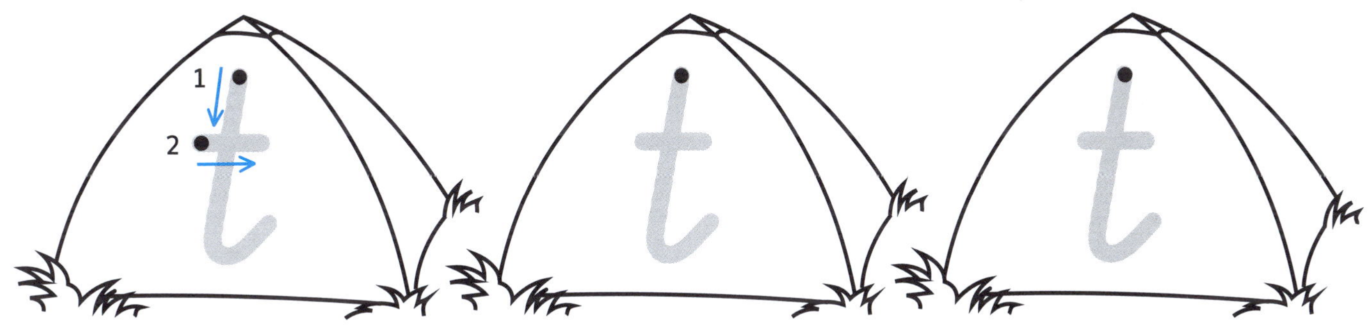

tent

Trace the letter.

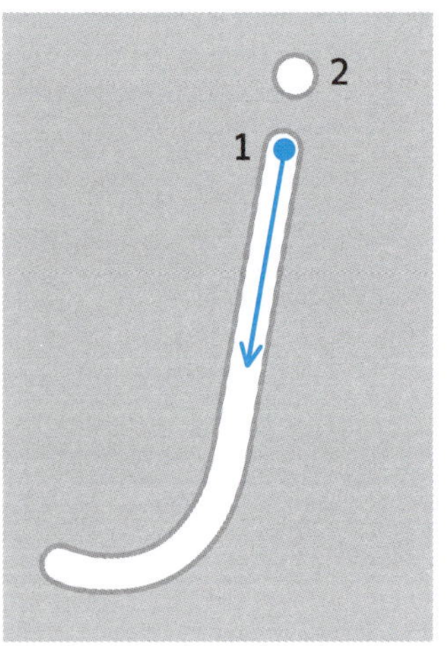

jam

Start at the dot. Follow the arrow.

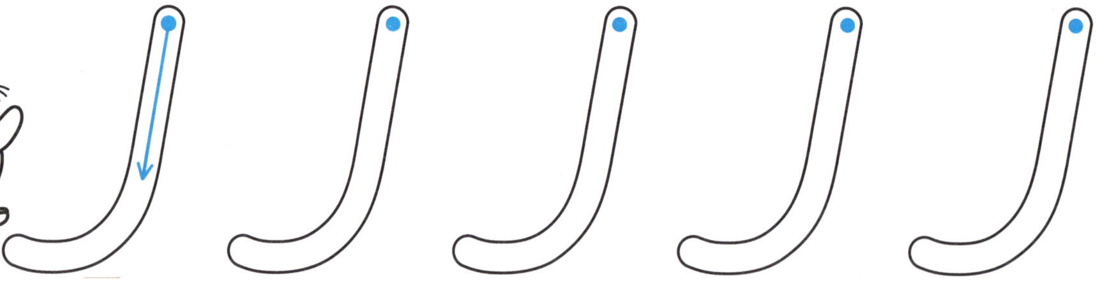

jump

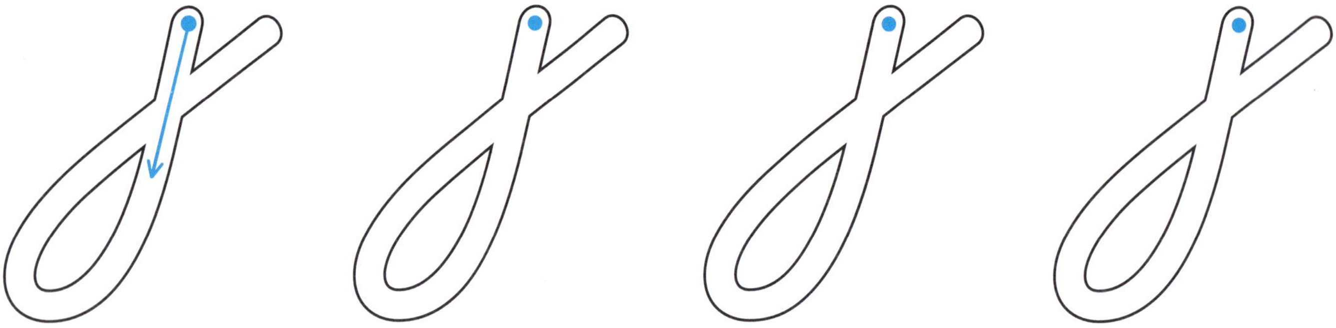

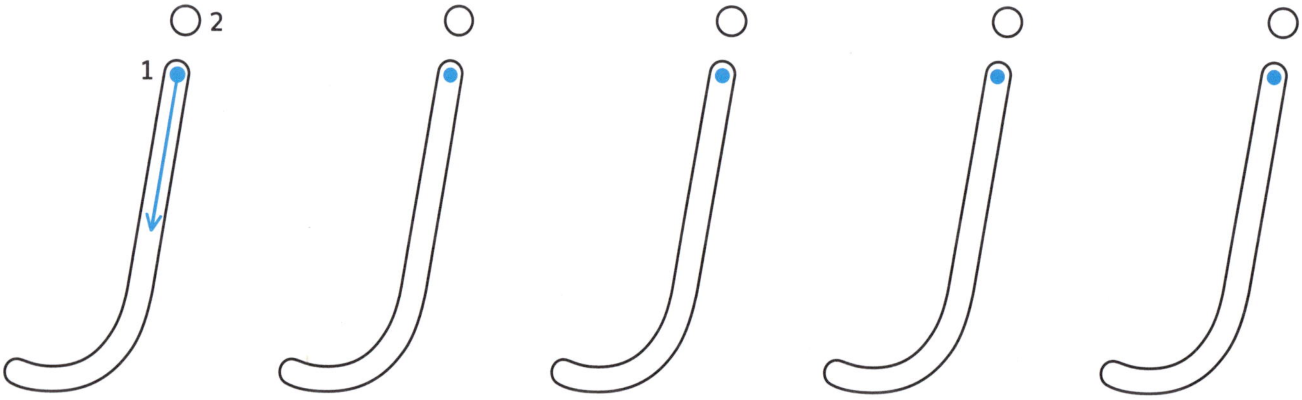

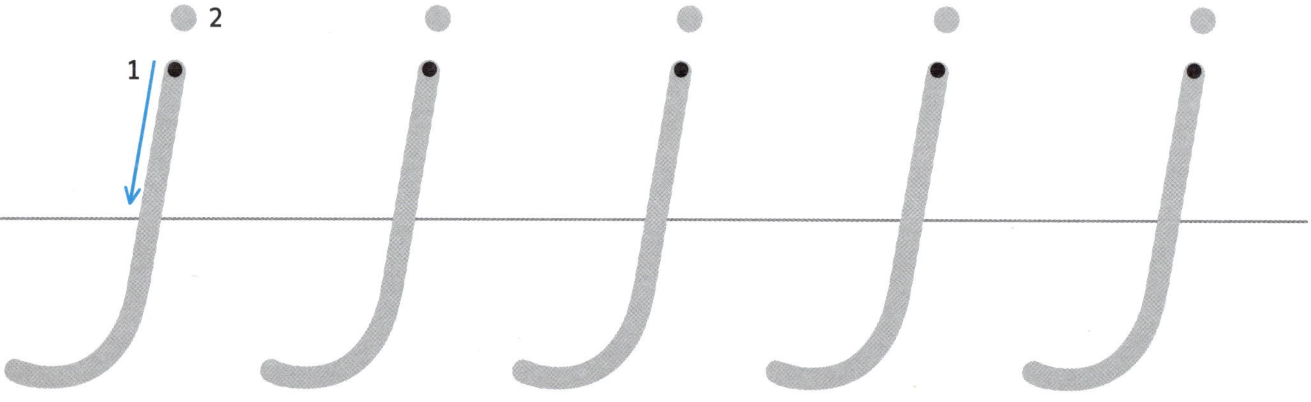

2
1

2
1

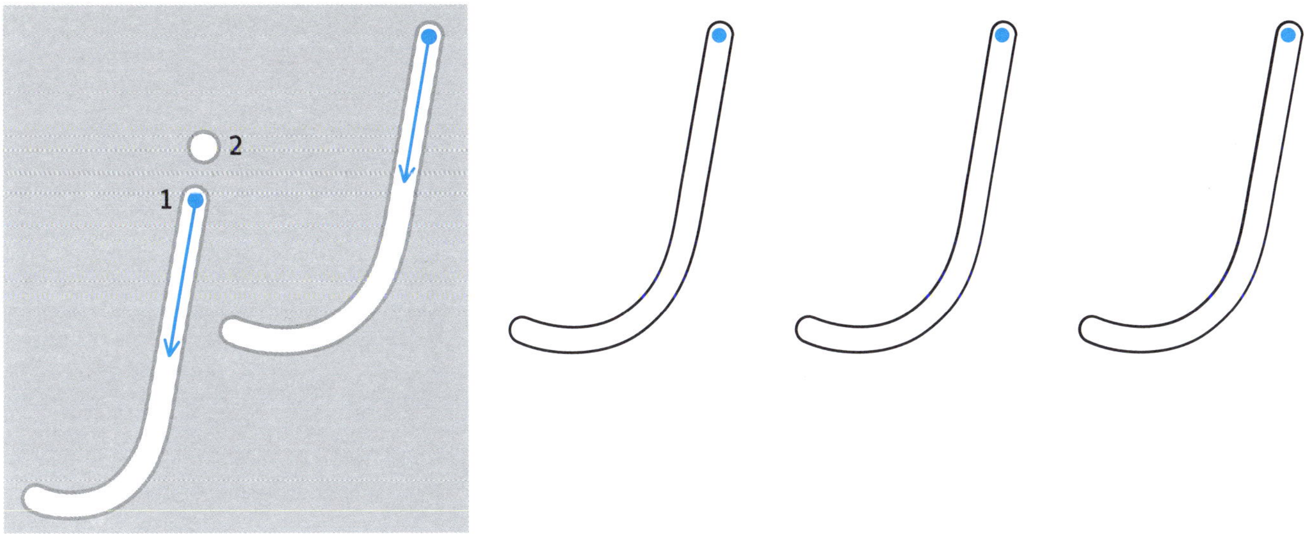

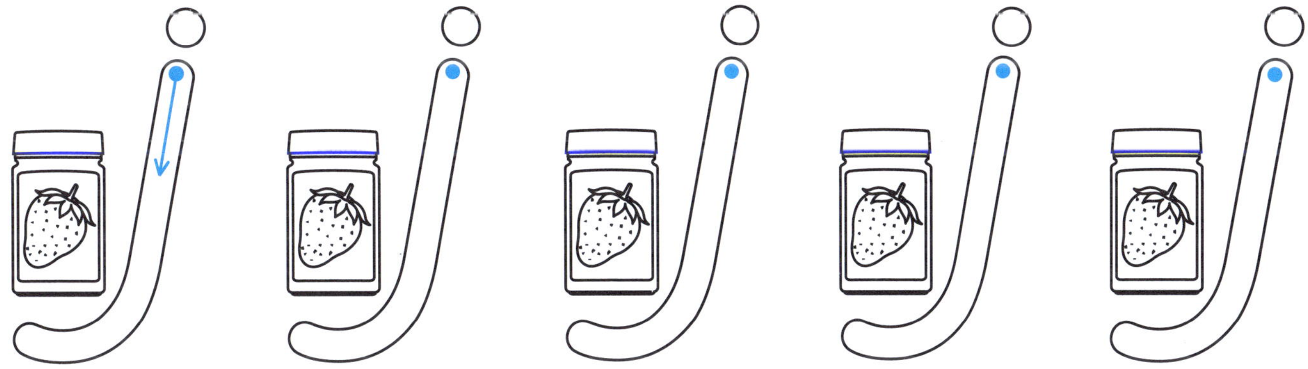

1
2

jam

jeans

get.ga/PMWA200

Trace the letter.

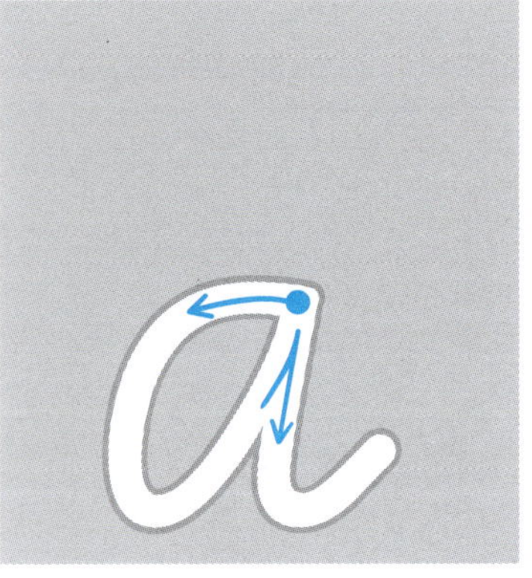

Start at the dot. Follow the arrow.

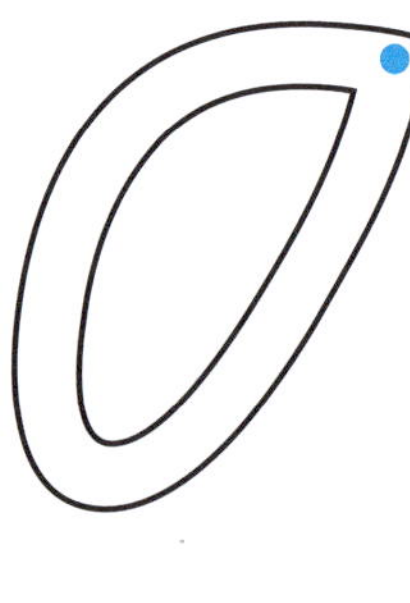
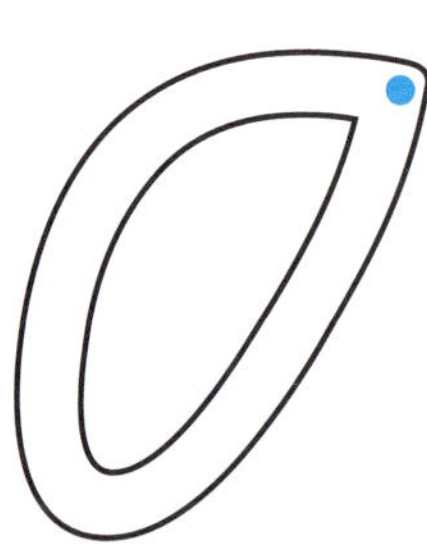

asleep

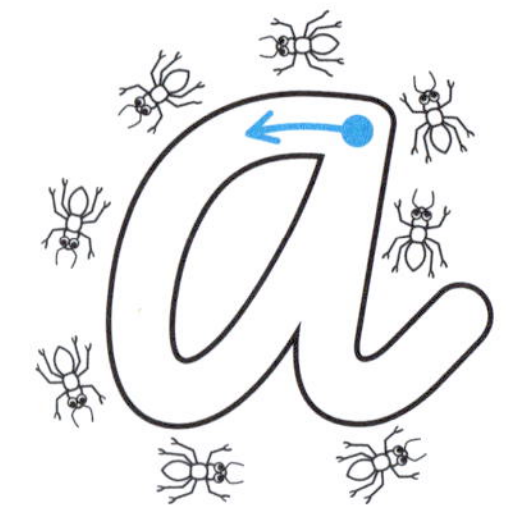

ants

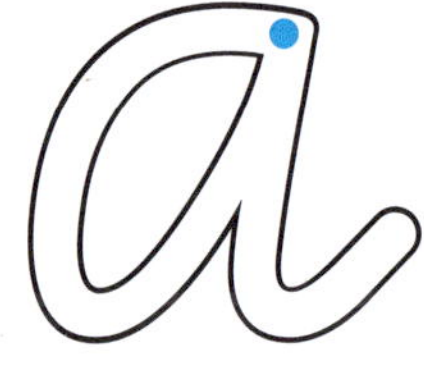

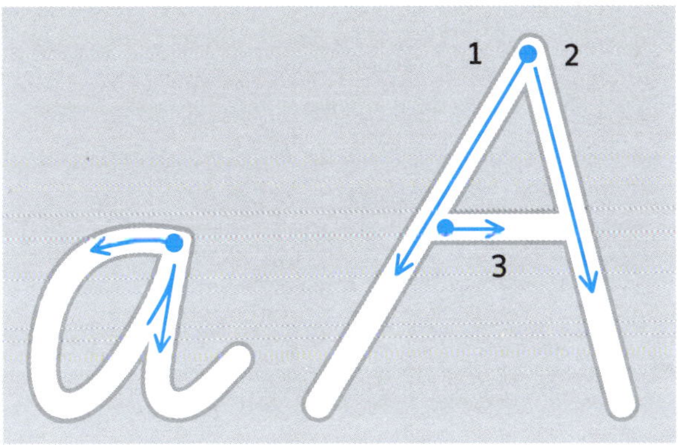

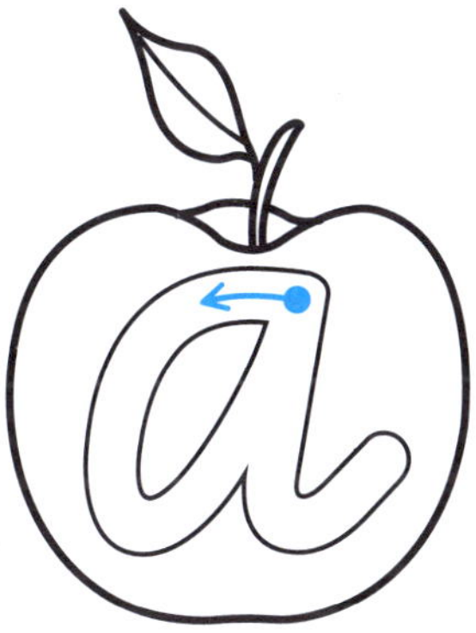

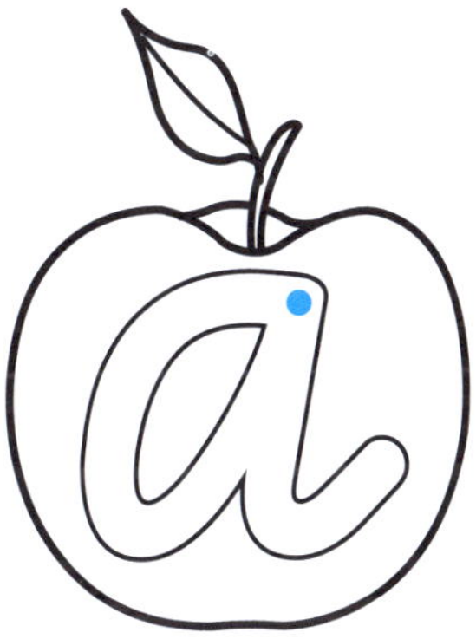

a A

1 2 3

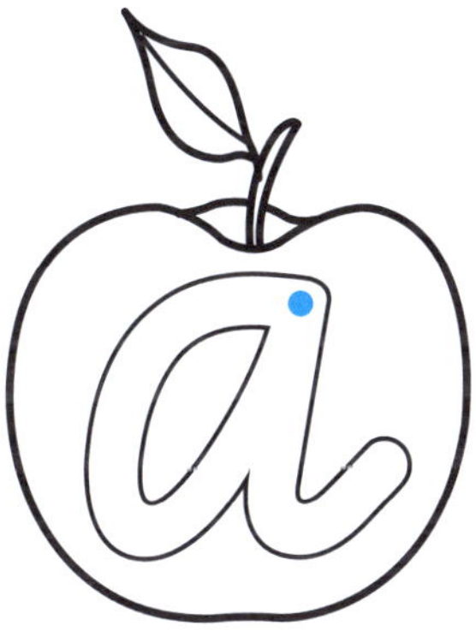

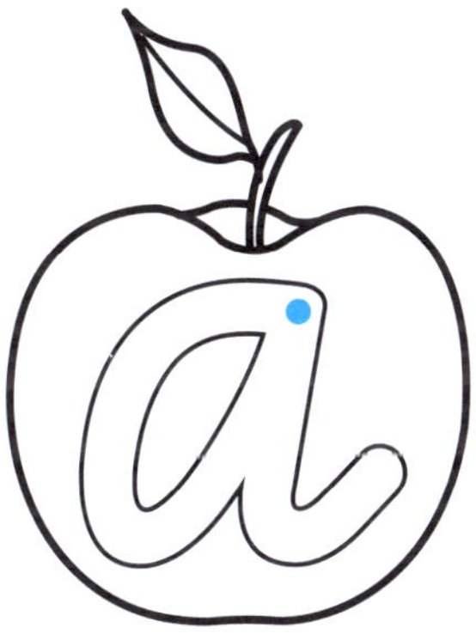

A A

apple

Trace the letter.

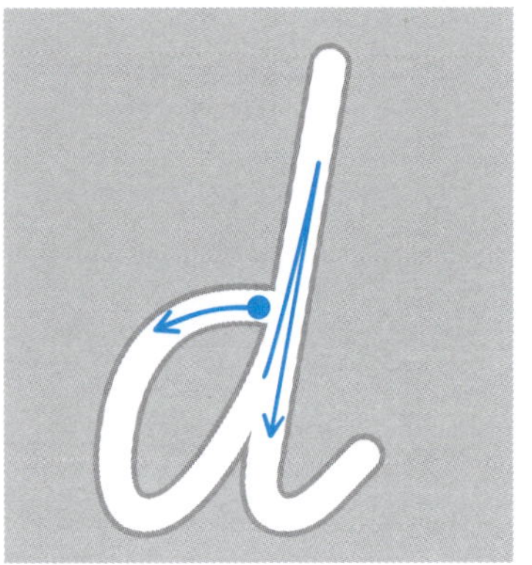

duck

Start at the dot. Follow the arrow.

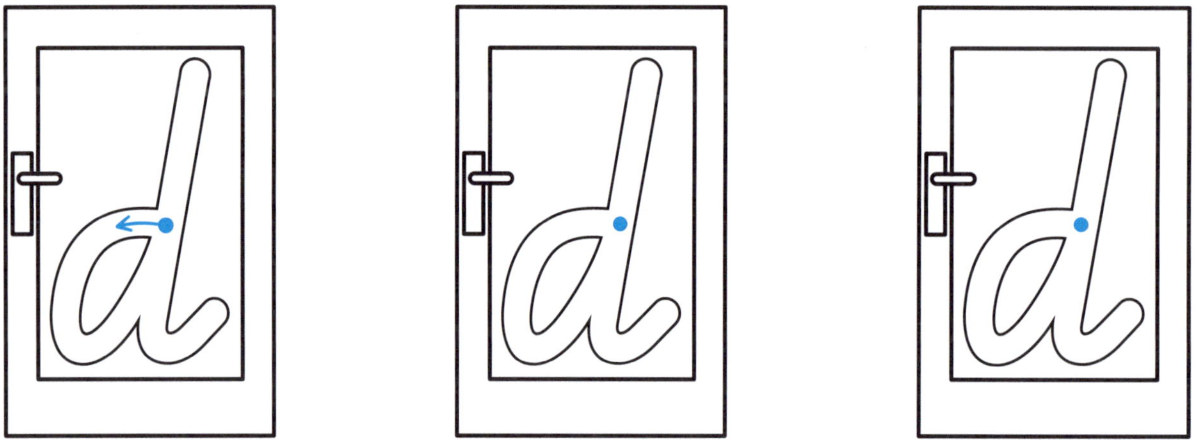

door

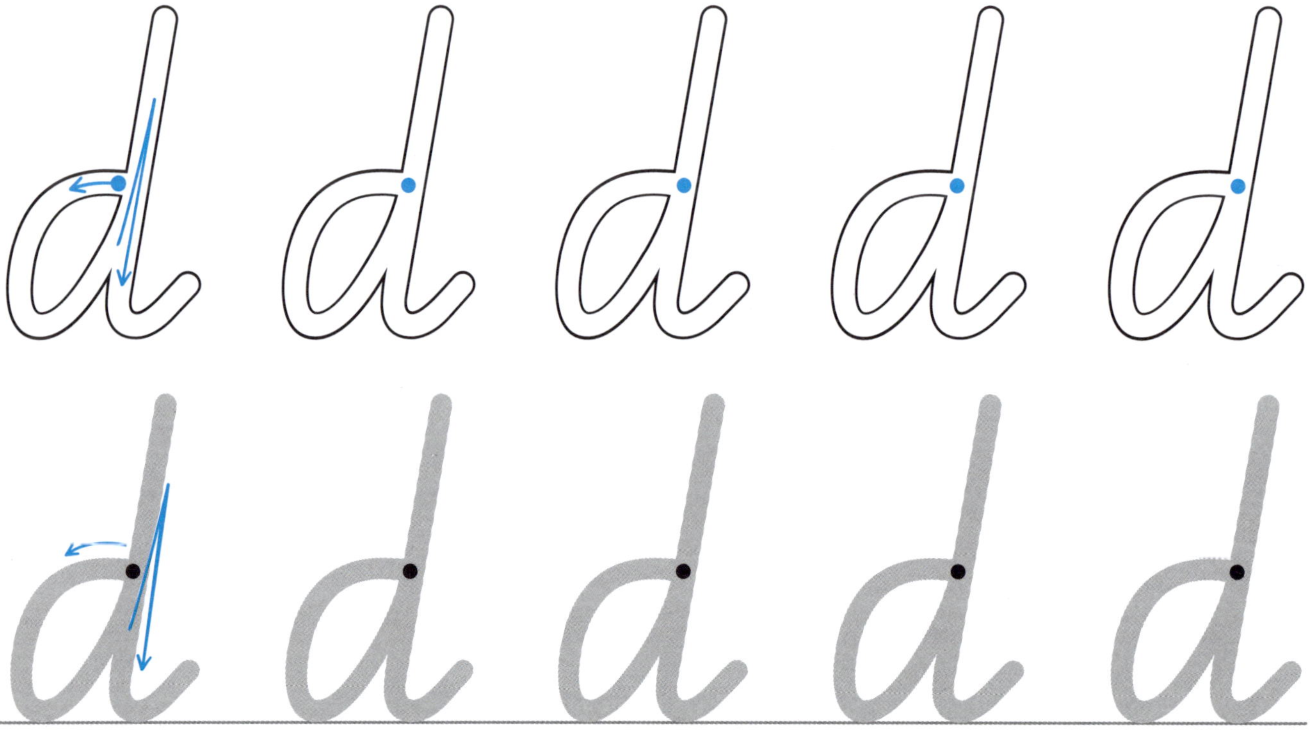

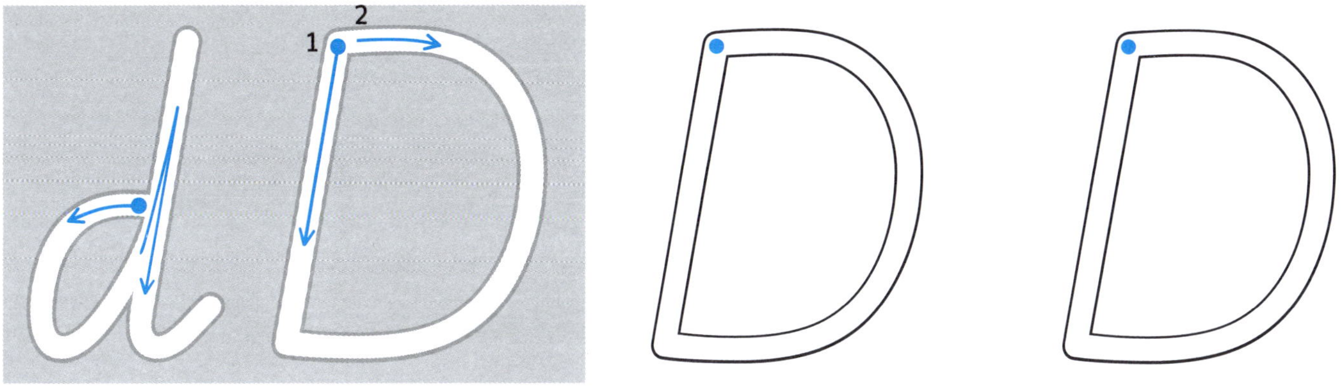

dog

dinosaur

Trace the letter.

gate

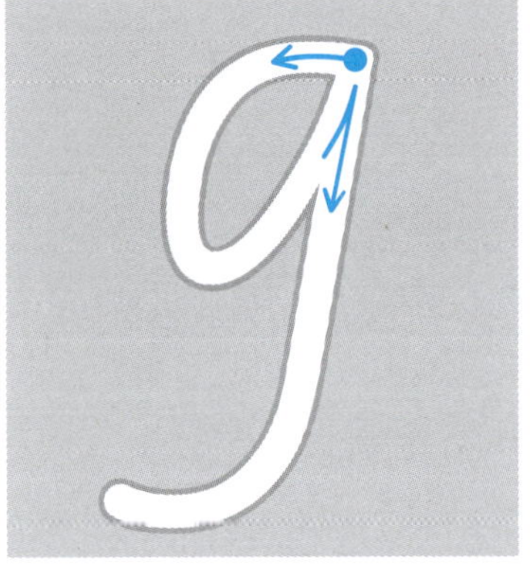

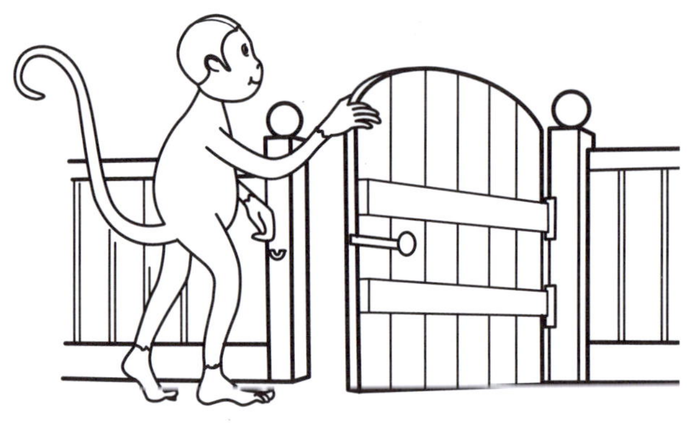

Start at the dot. Follow the arrow.

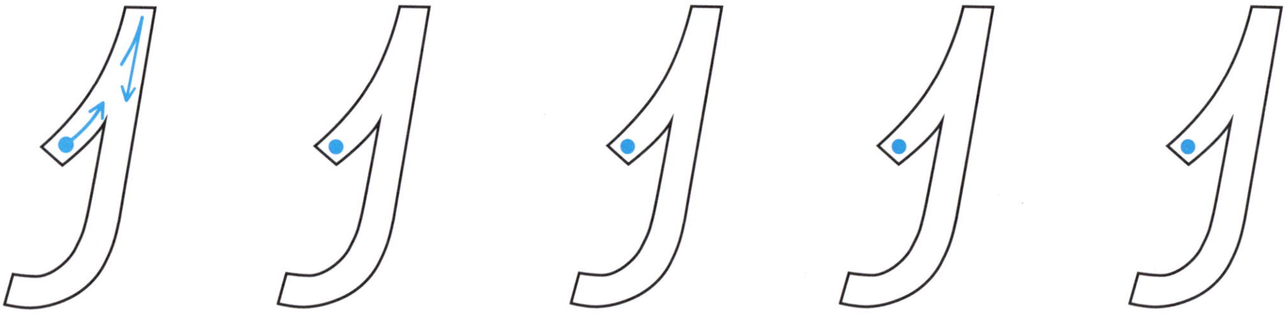

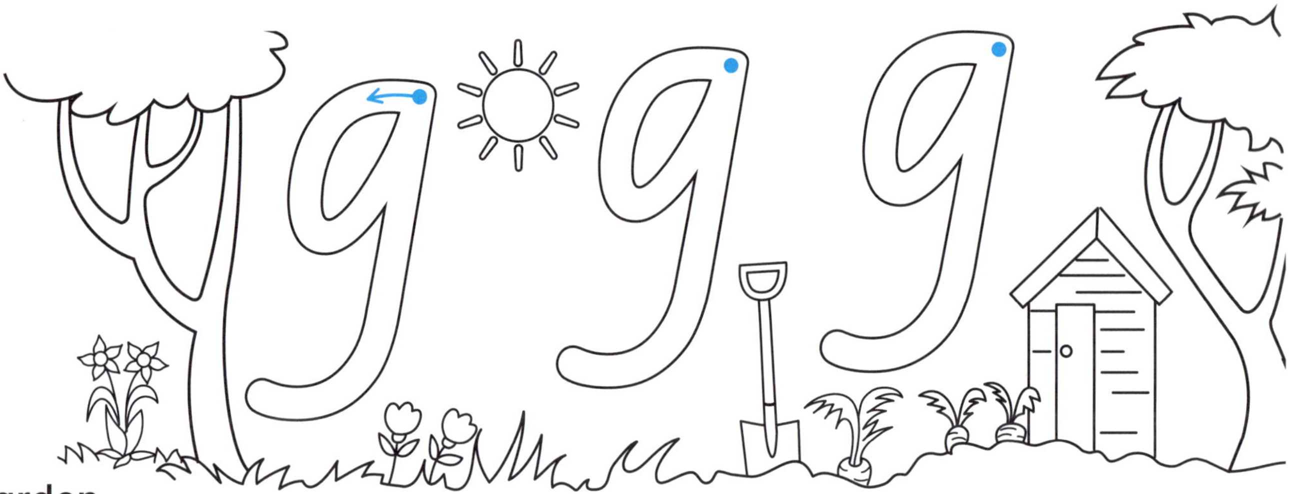

garden

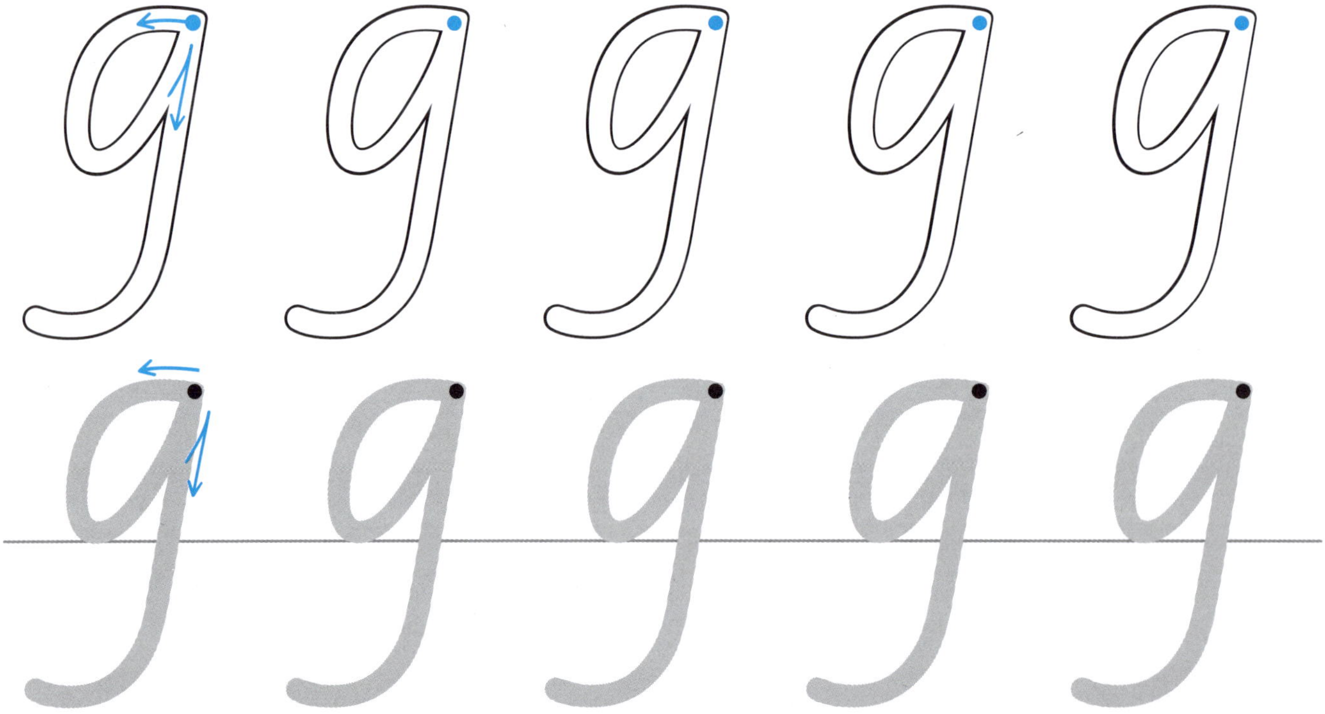

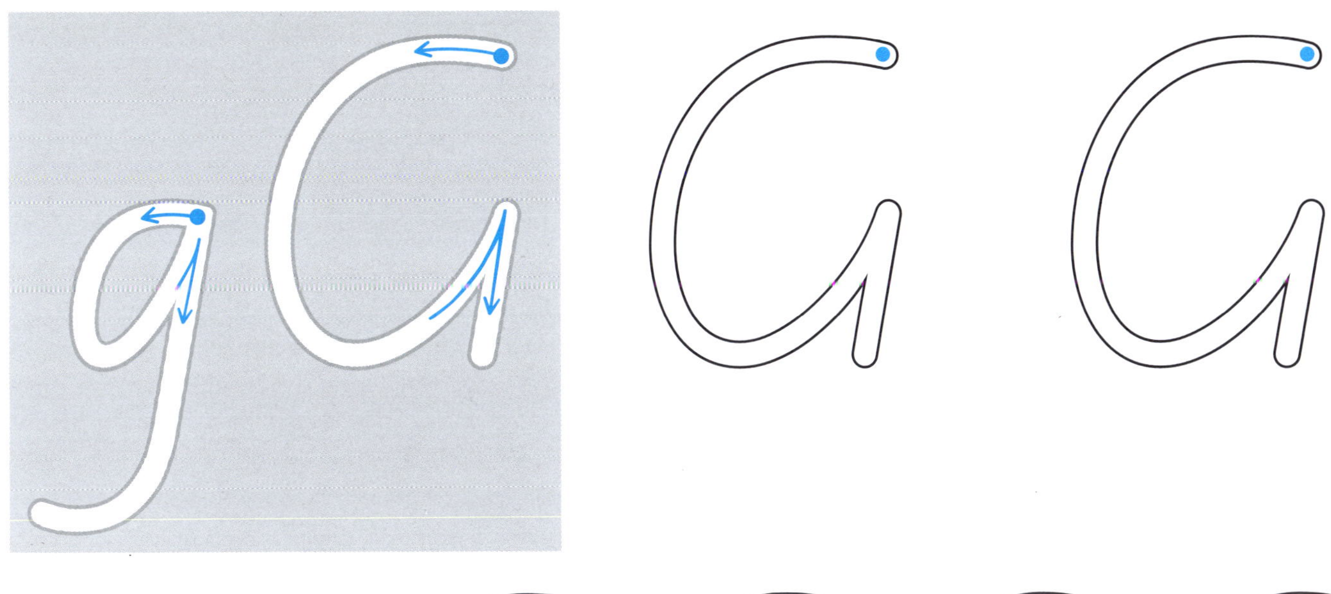

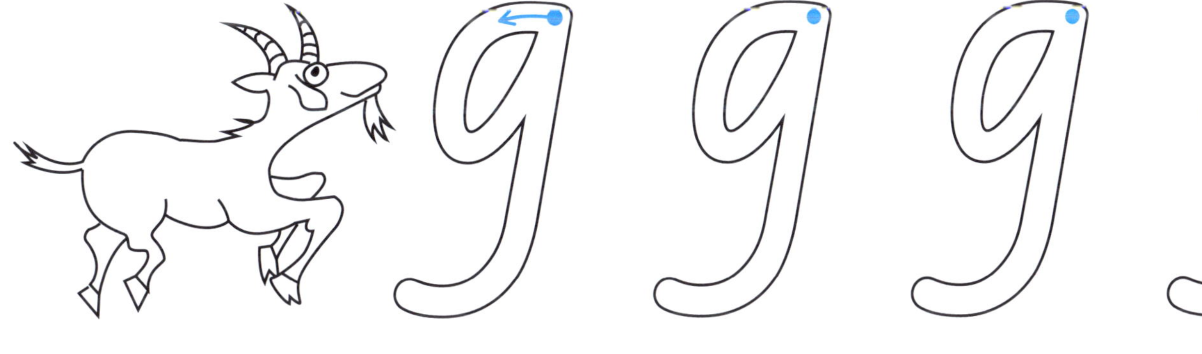

goat

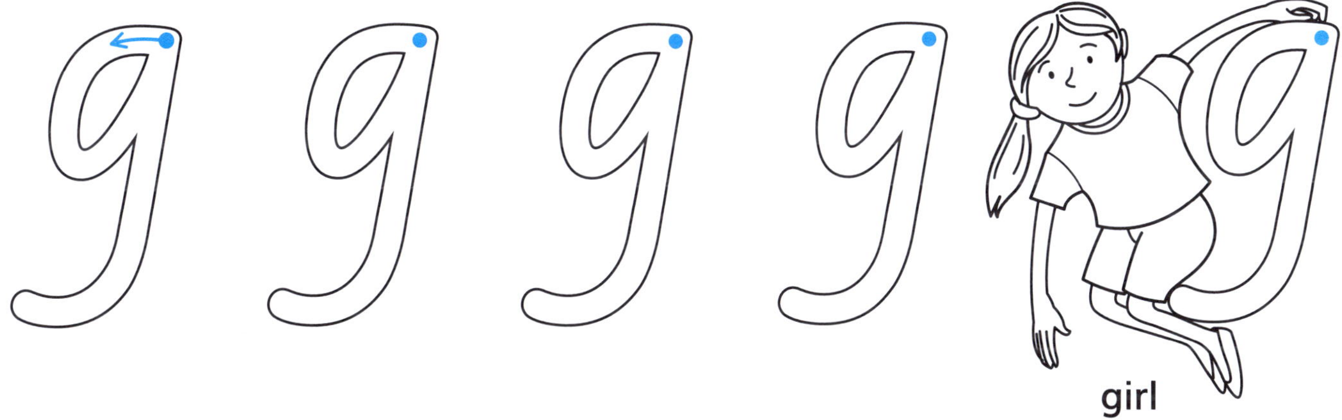

girl

Trace the letter.

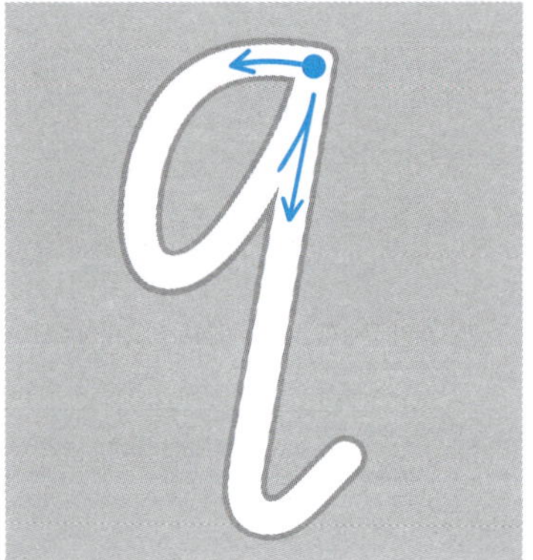

queen

Start at the dot. Follow the arrow.

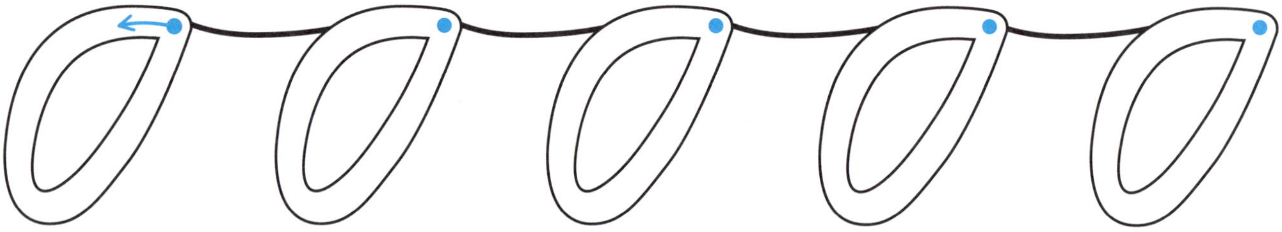

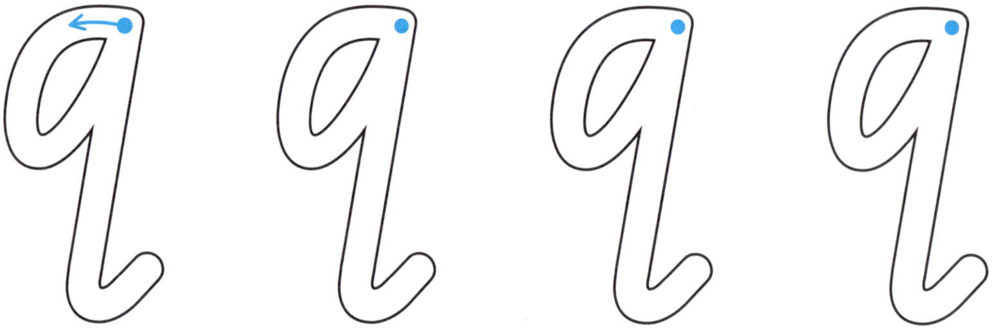

queen

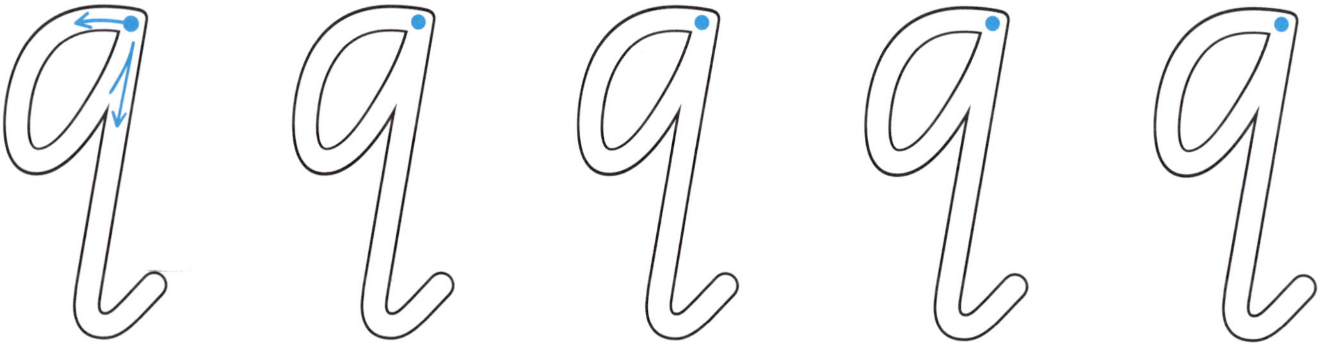

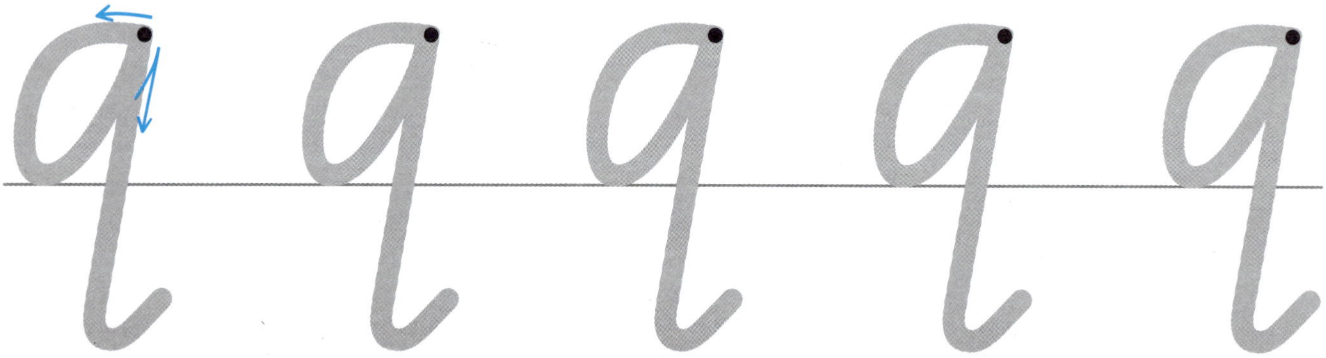

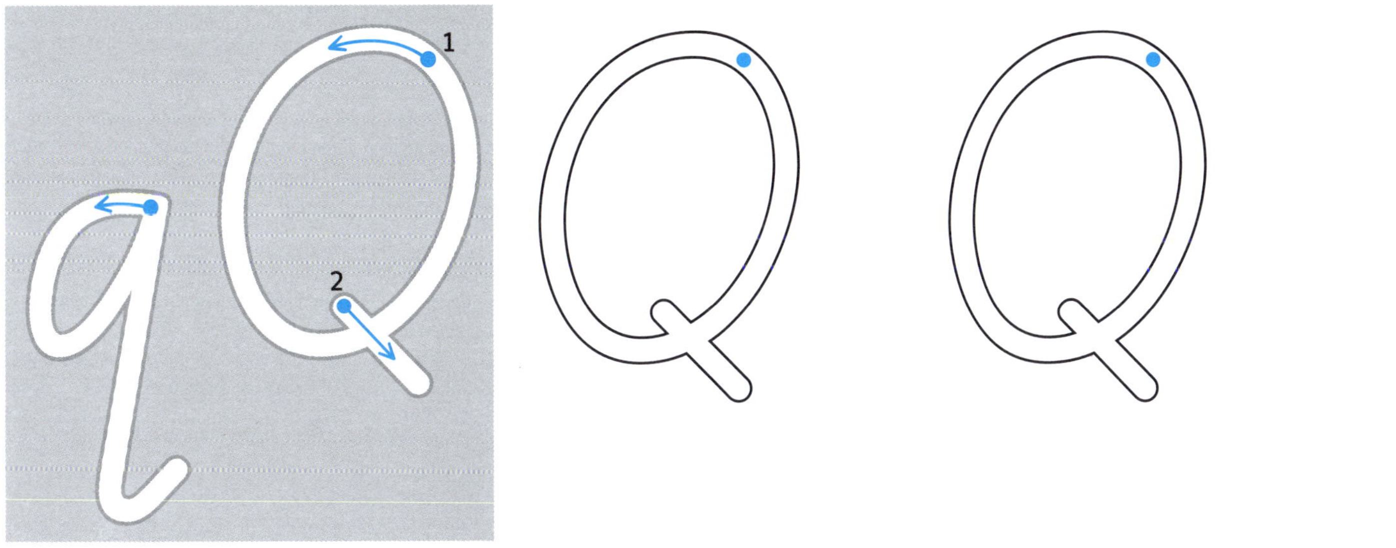

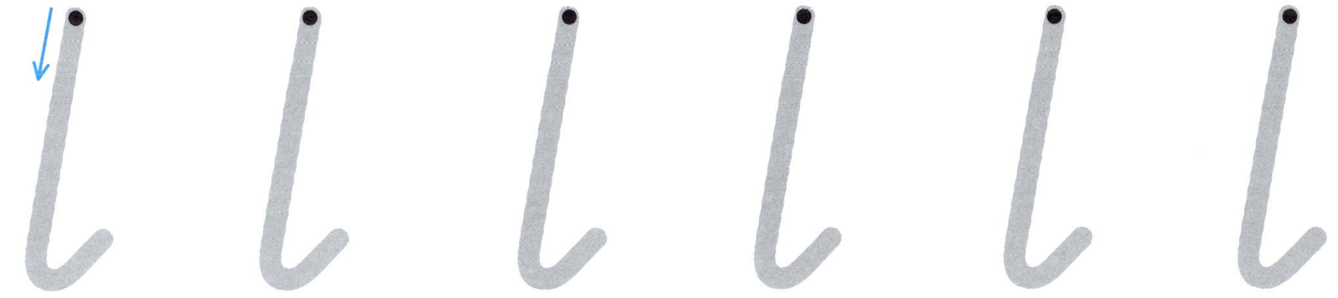

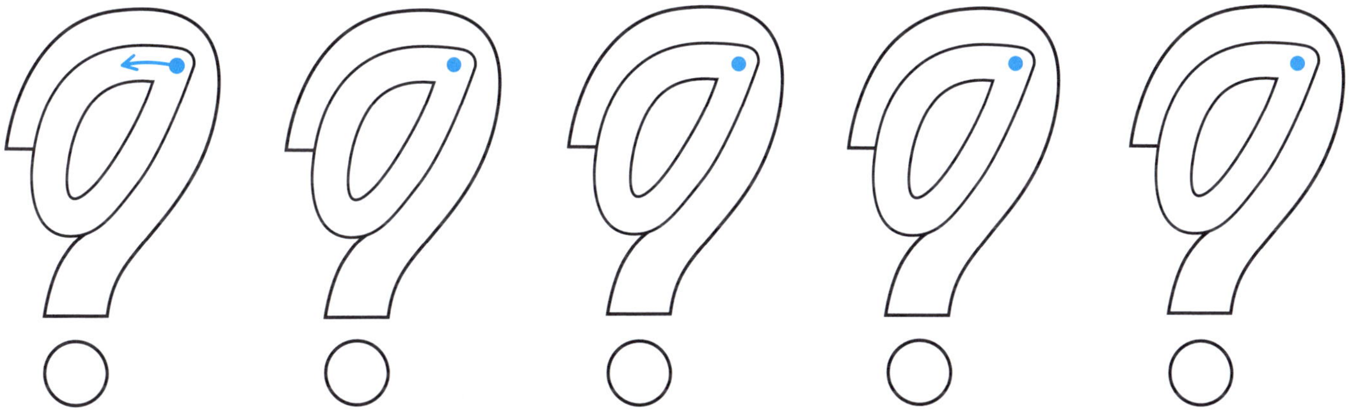

question mark

Trace the letter.

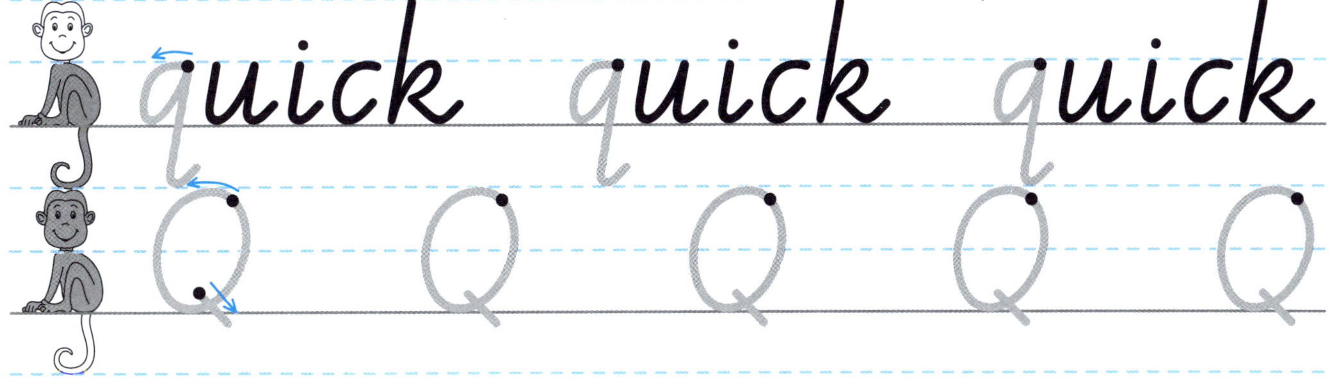

ISBN: 9780170421416

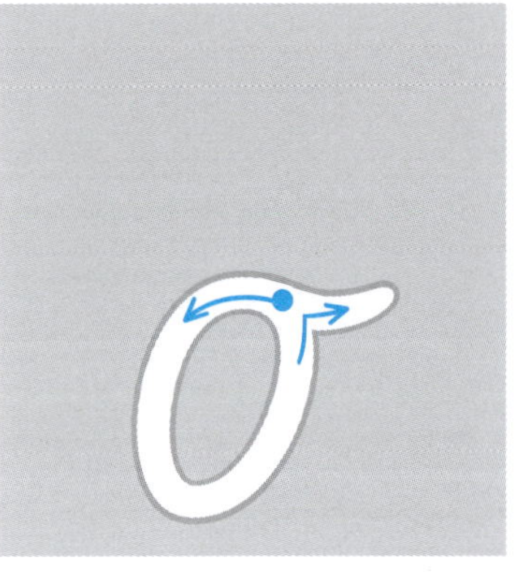

outside

Start at the dot. Follow the arrow.

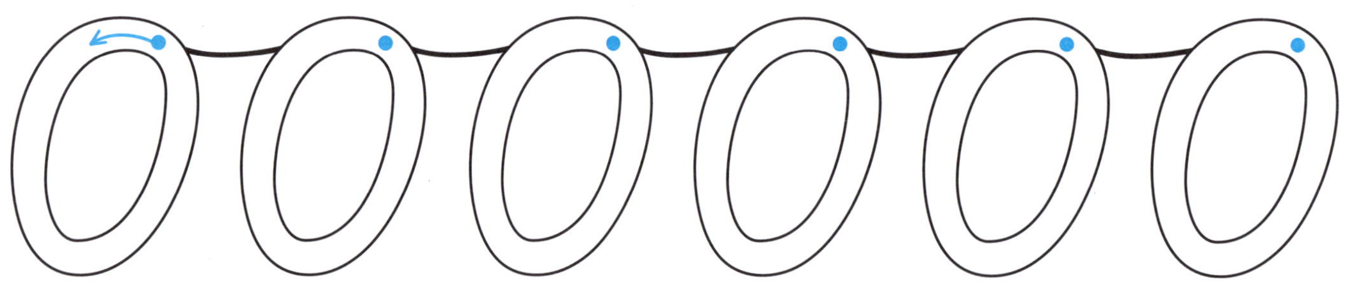

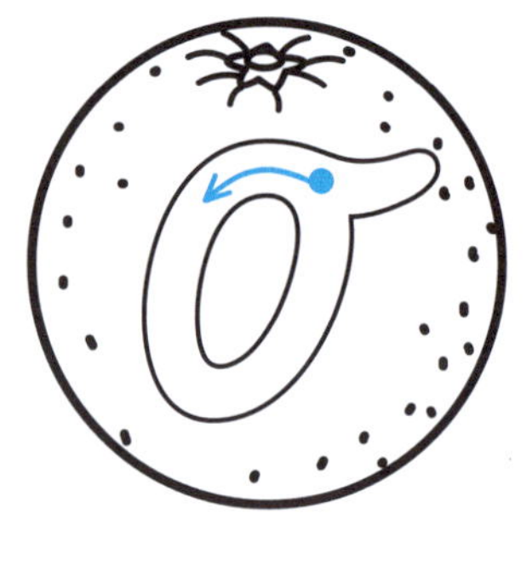

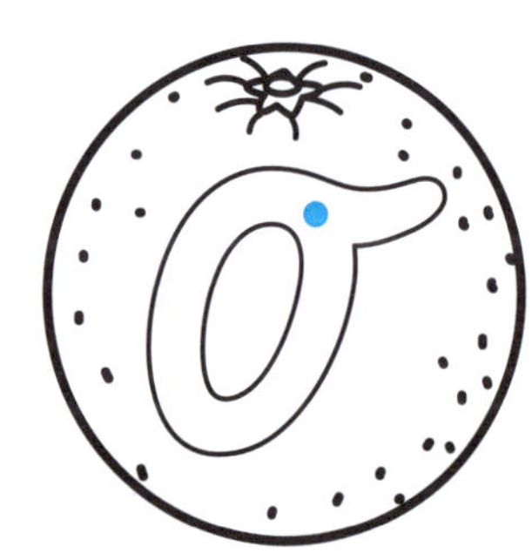

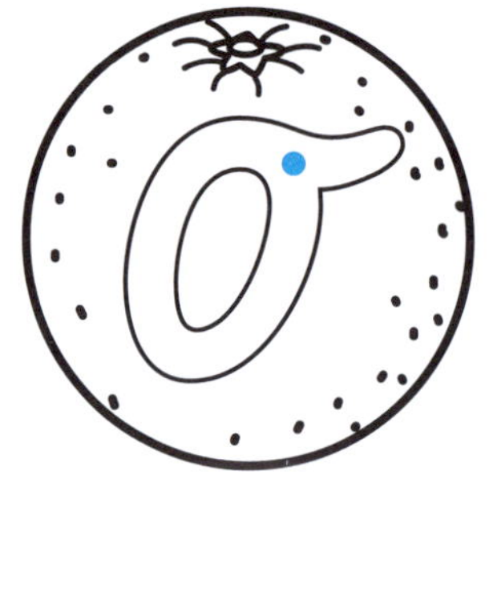

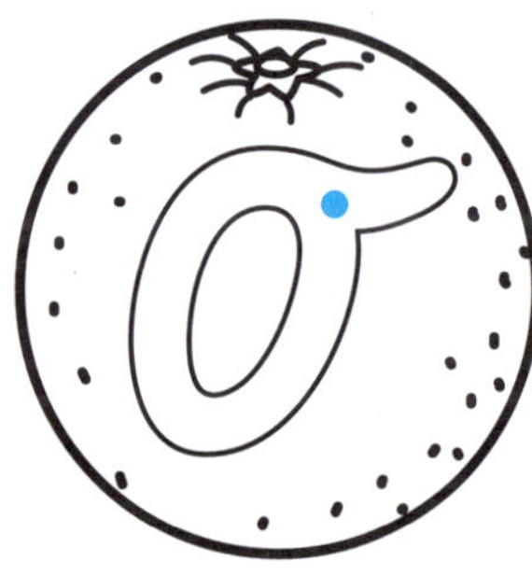

orange

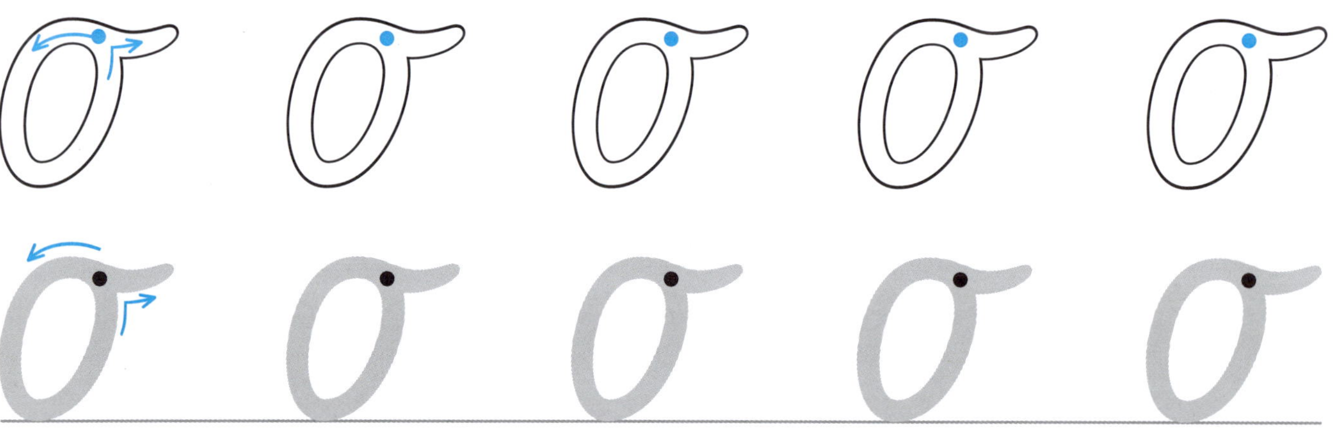

ISBN: 9780170421416

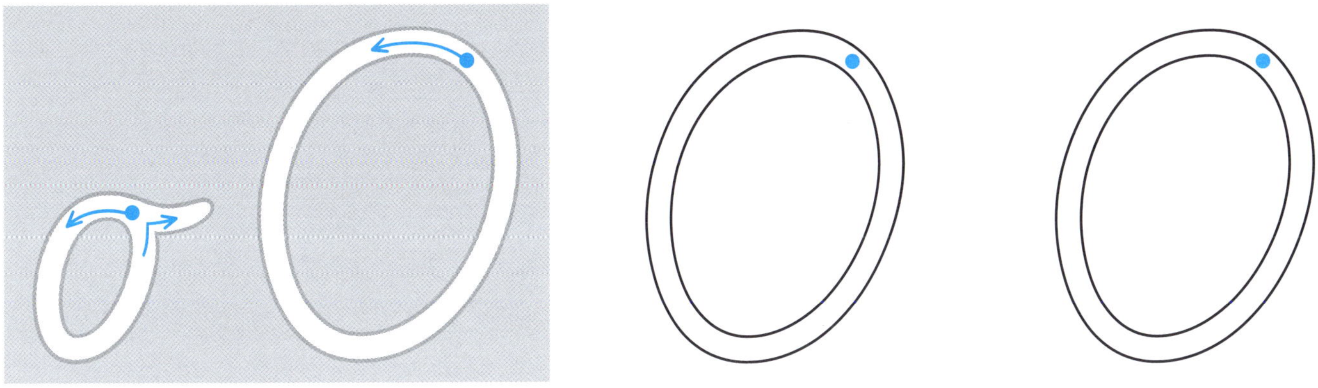

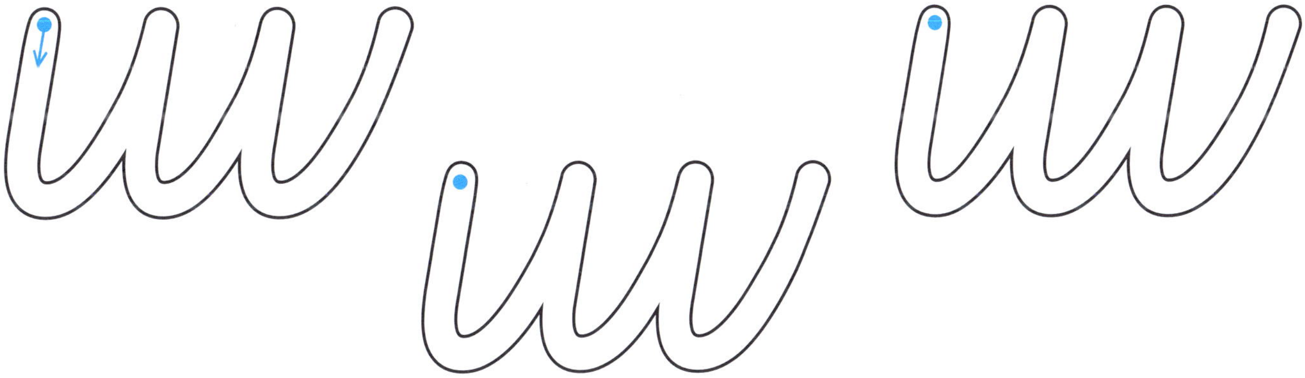

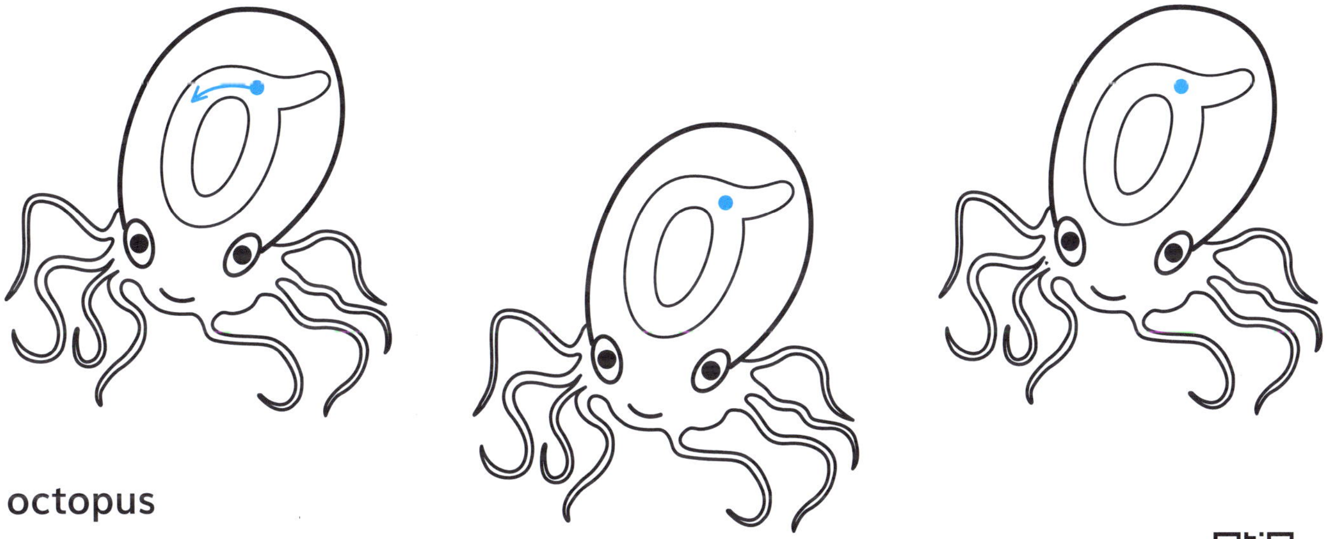

octopus

Trace the letter.

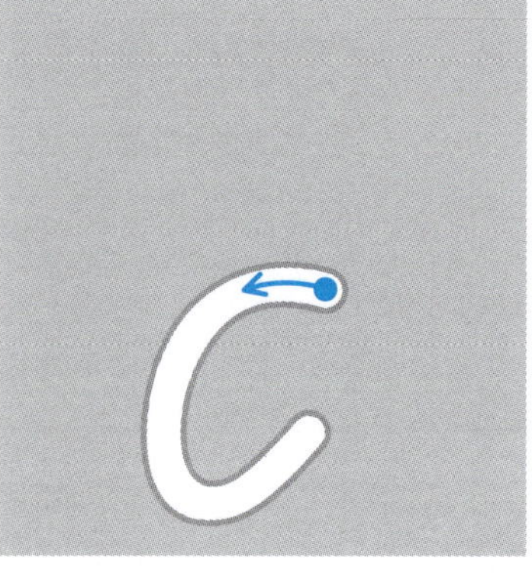

caterpillar

Start at the dot. Follow the arrow.

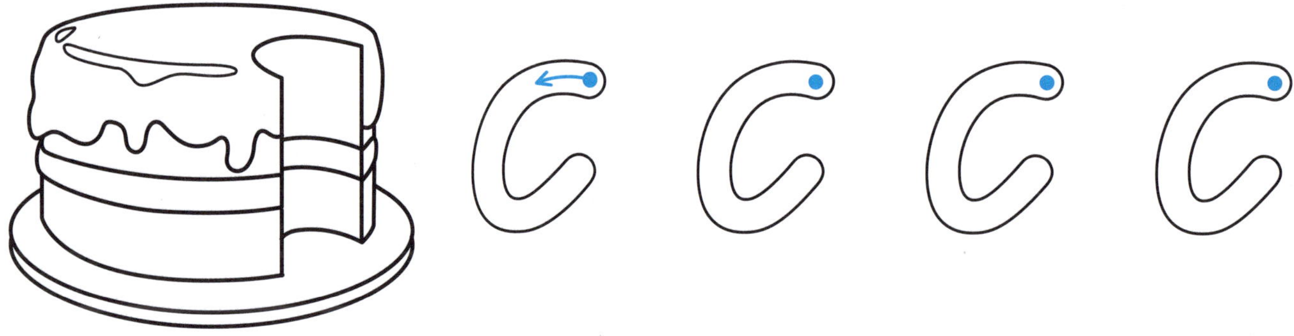

cake

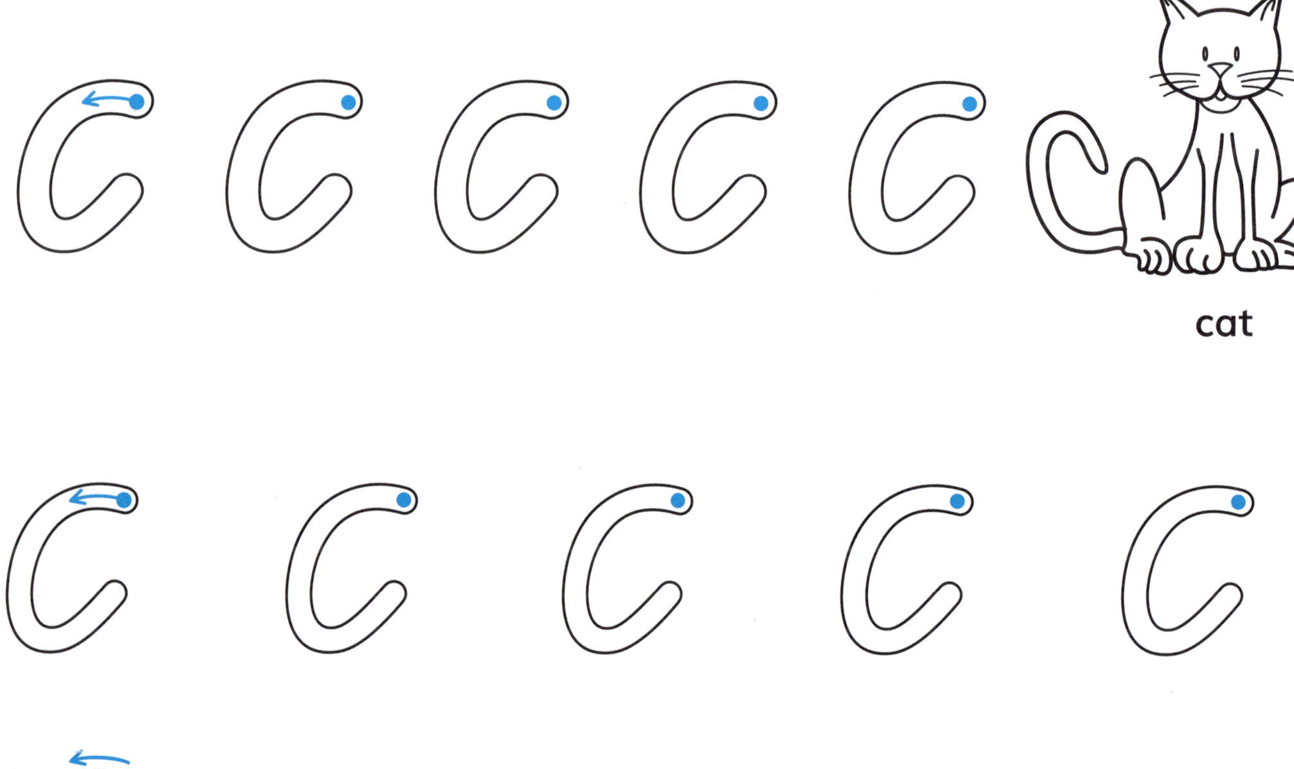

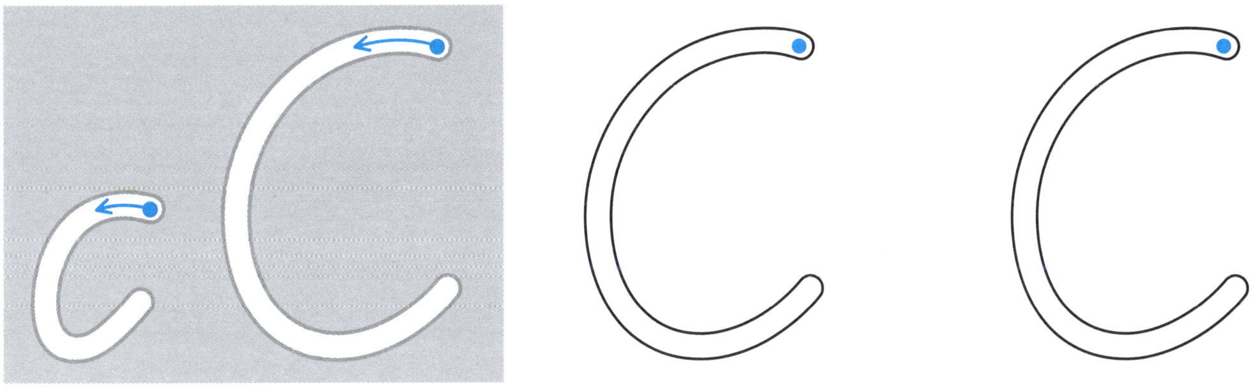

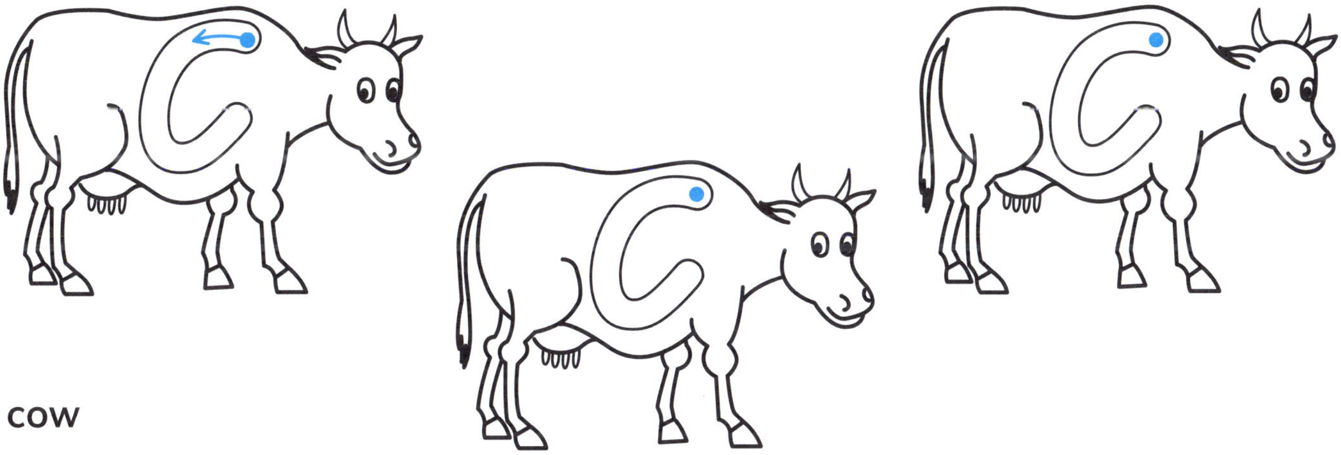

cow

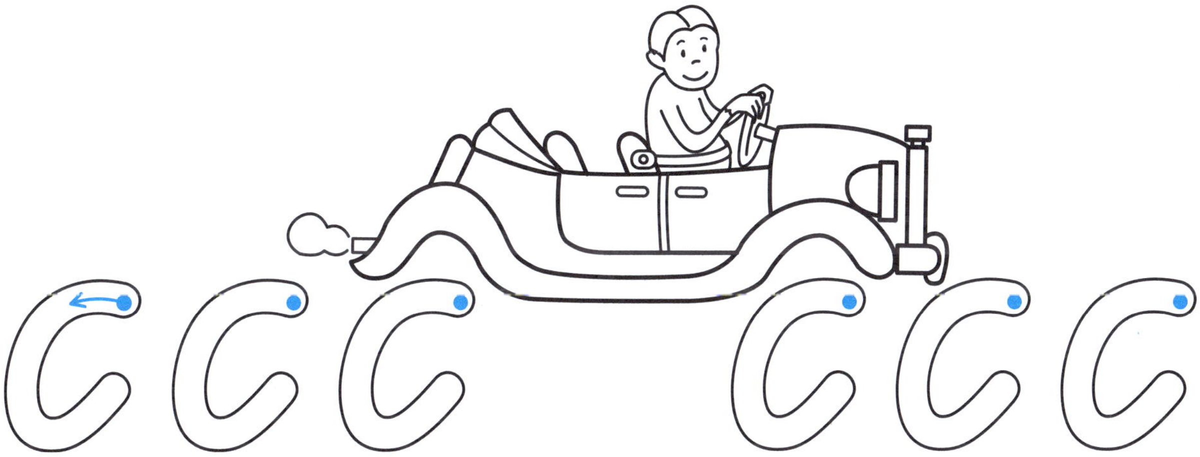

car

Trace the letter.

can can can can

c c c c c c

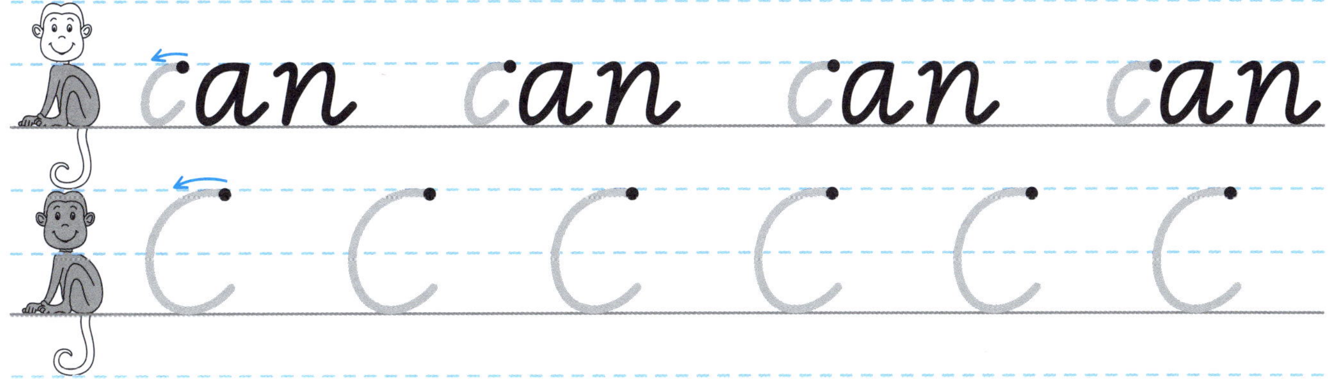

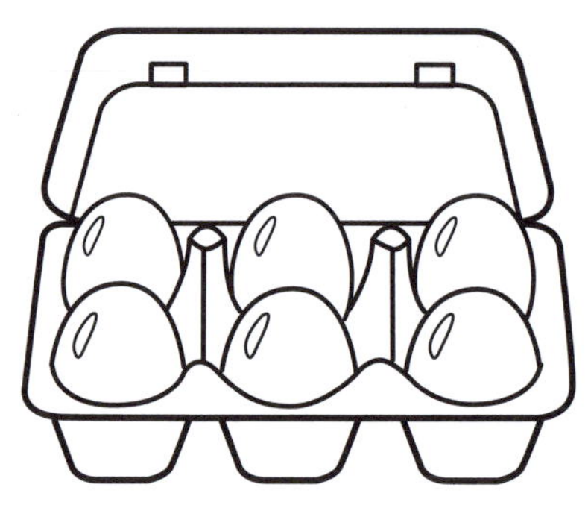

Start at the dot. Follow the arrow.

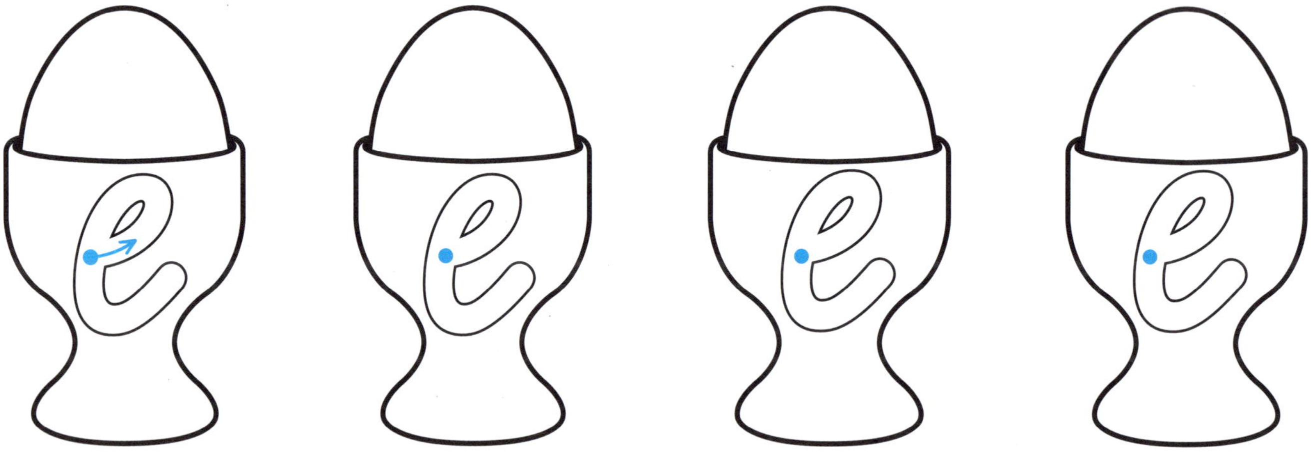

ele ele

egg

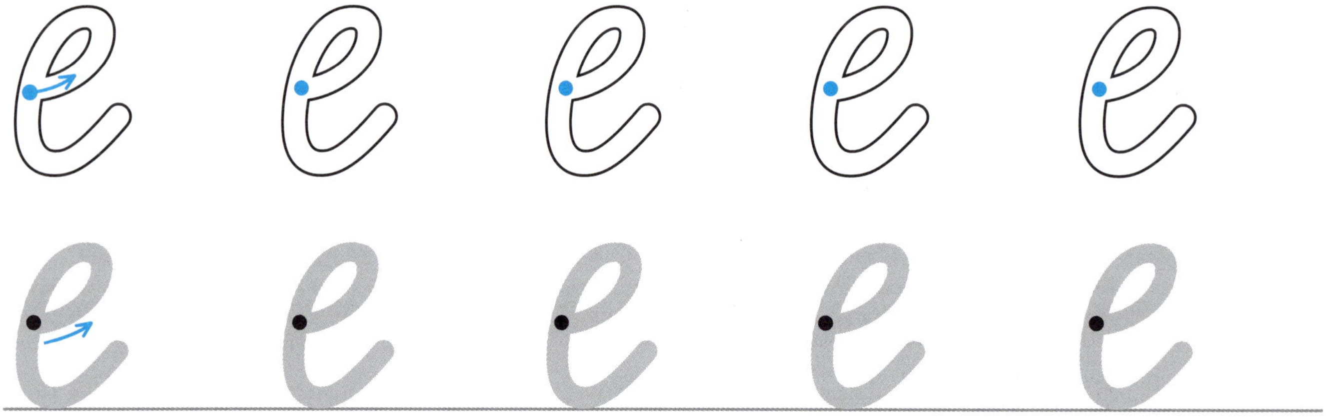

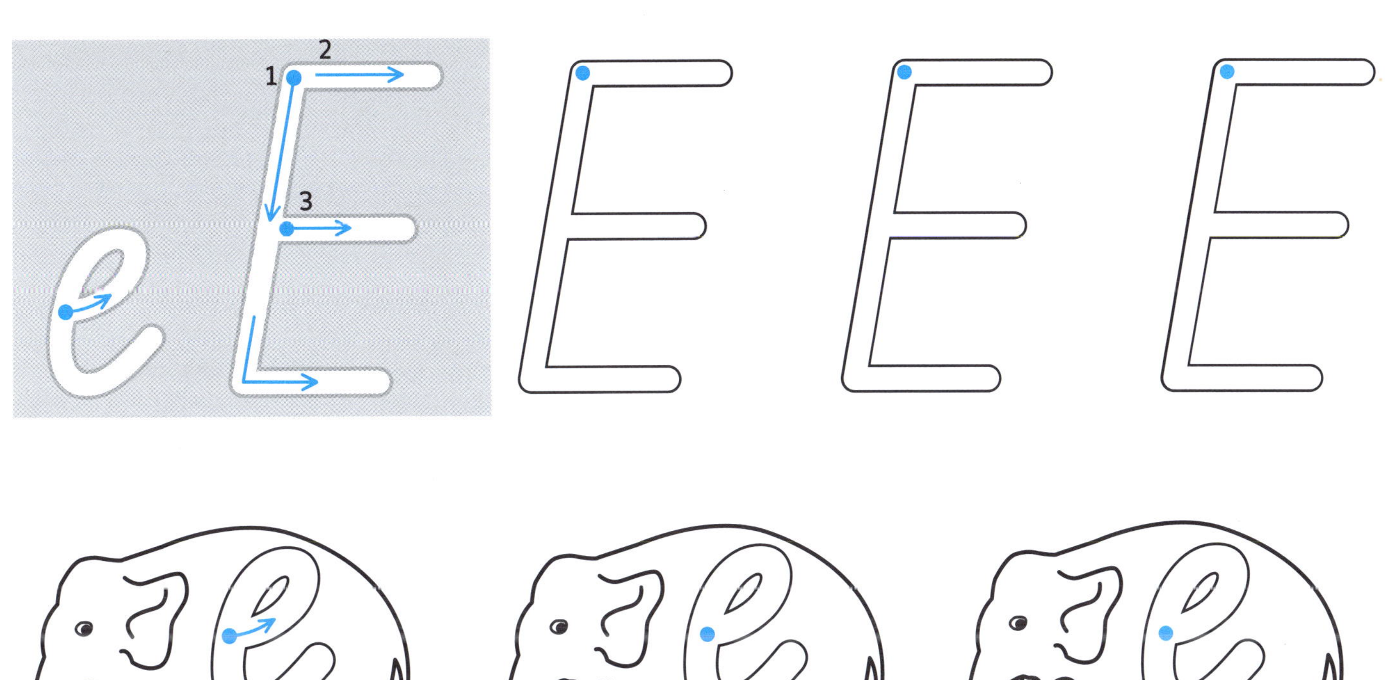

elephant

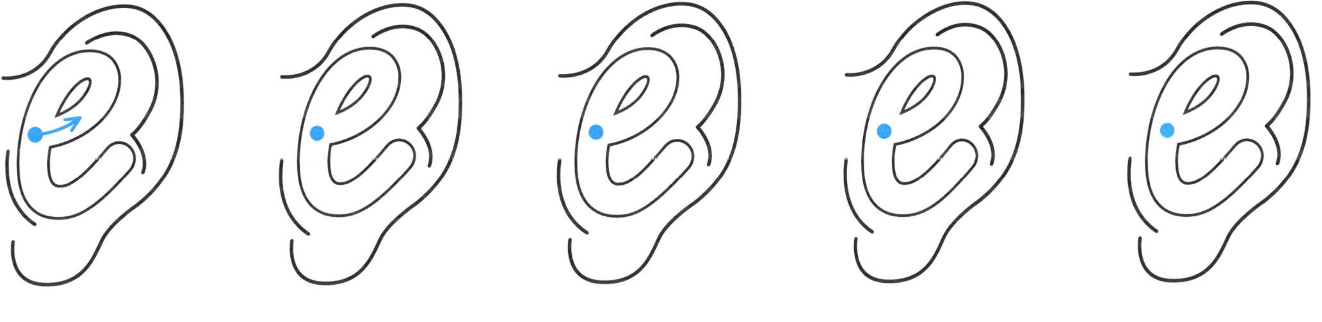

ear

Trace the letter.

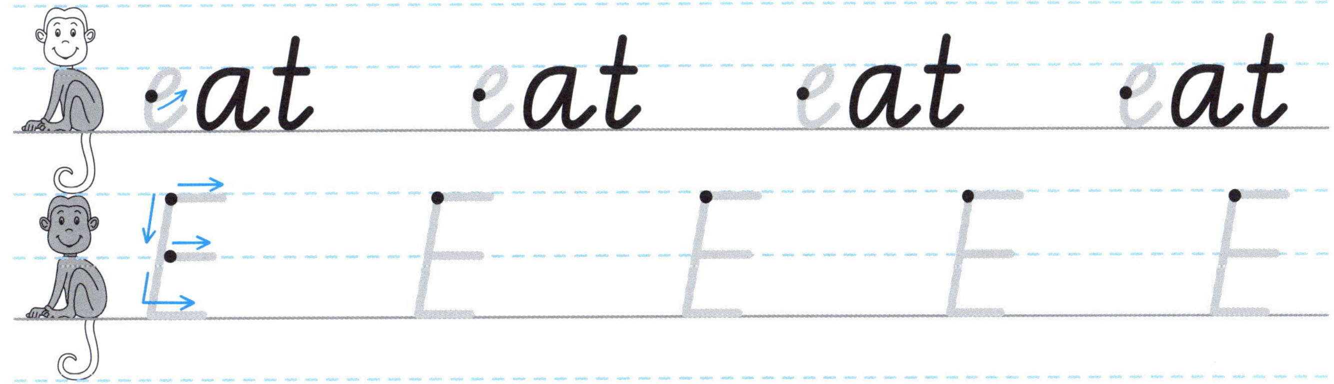

ISBN: 9780170421416

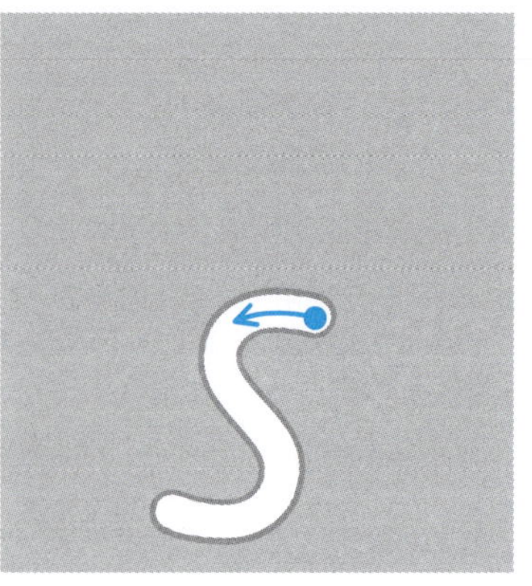

sun

Start at the dot. Follow the arrow.

snake

sun

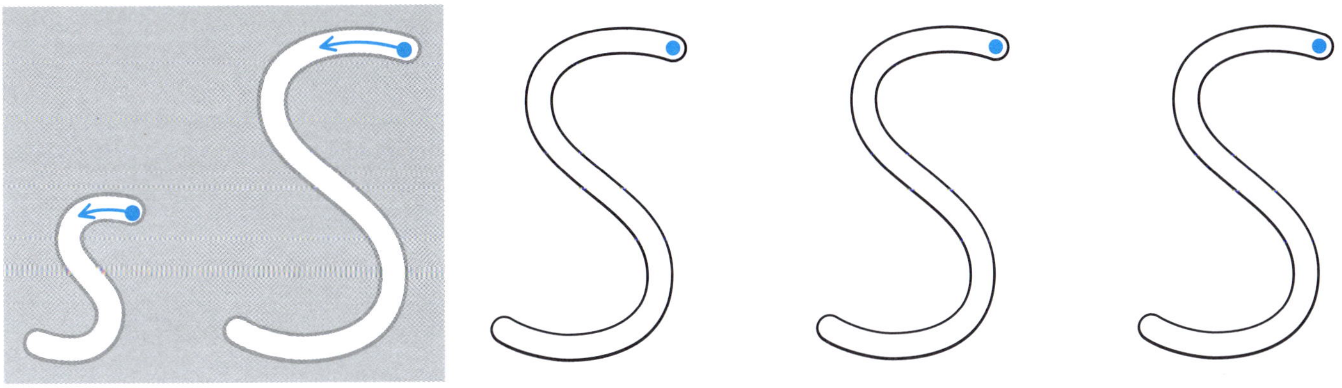

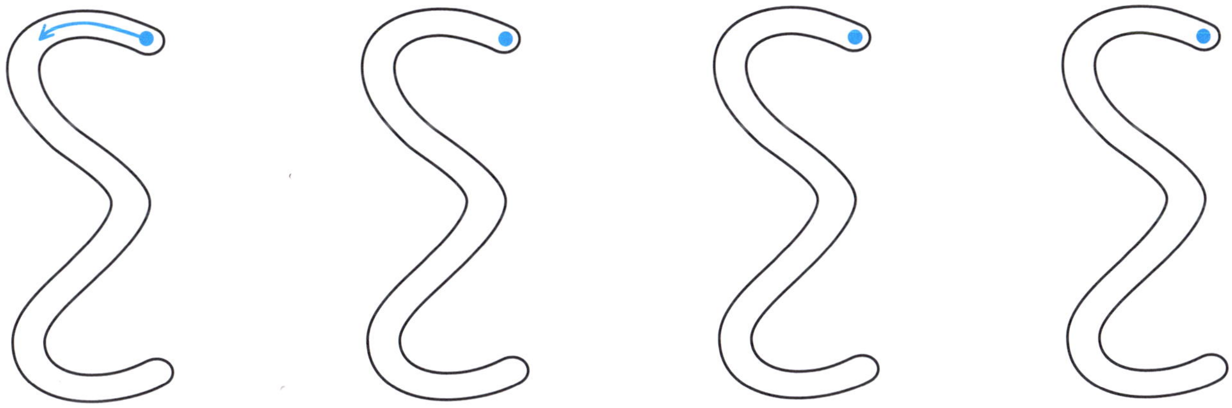

splash

Trace the letter.

ISBN: 9780170421416

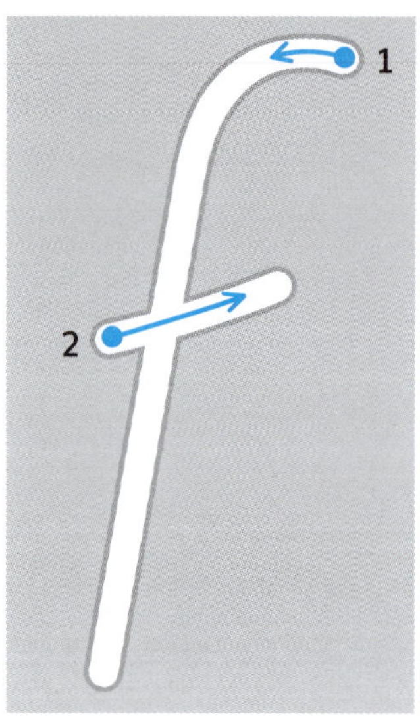

fish

Start at the dot. Follow the arrow.

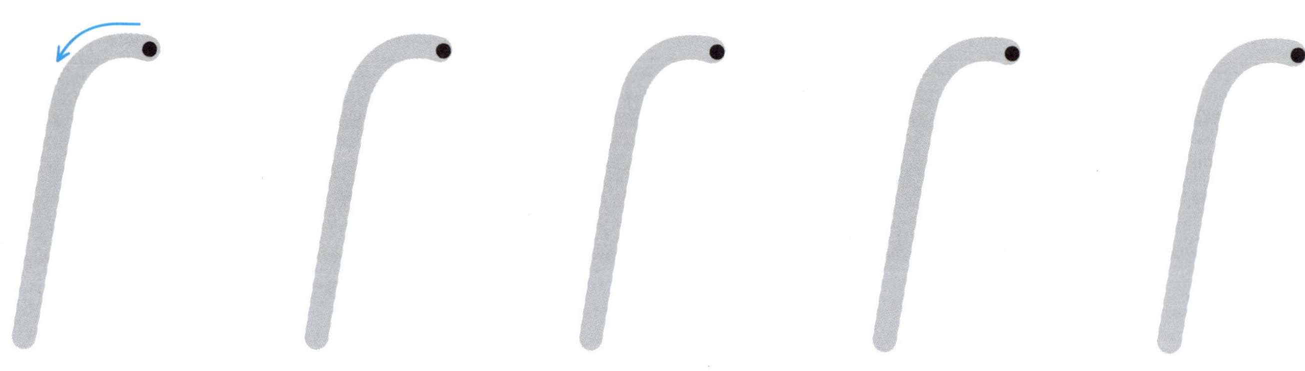

feather

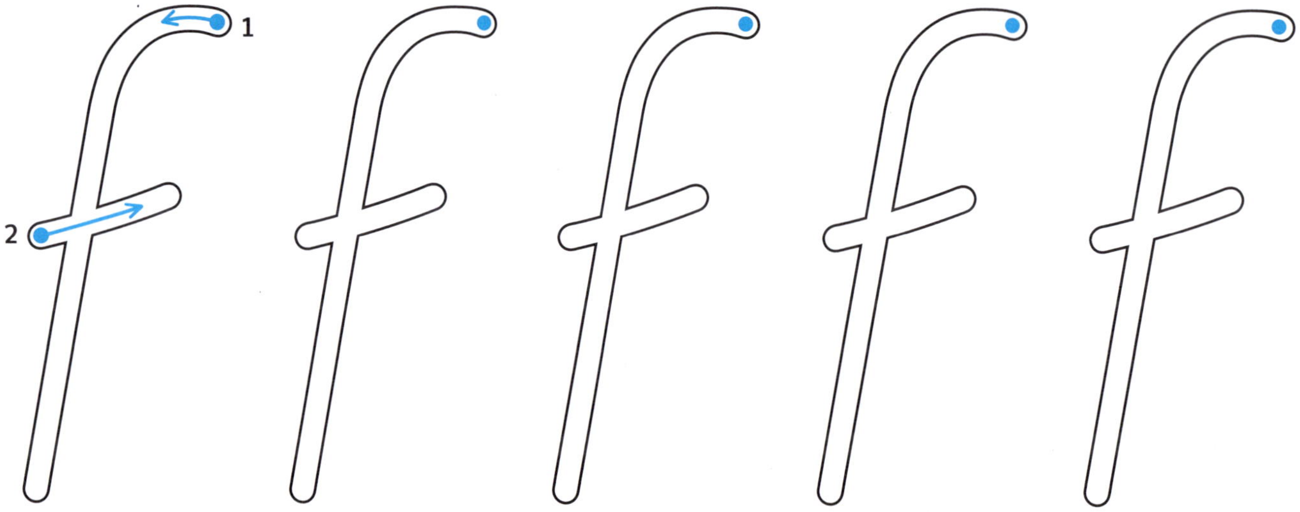

1

2

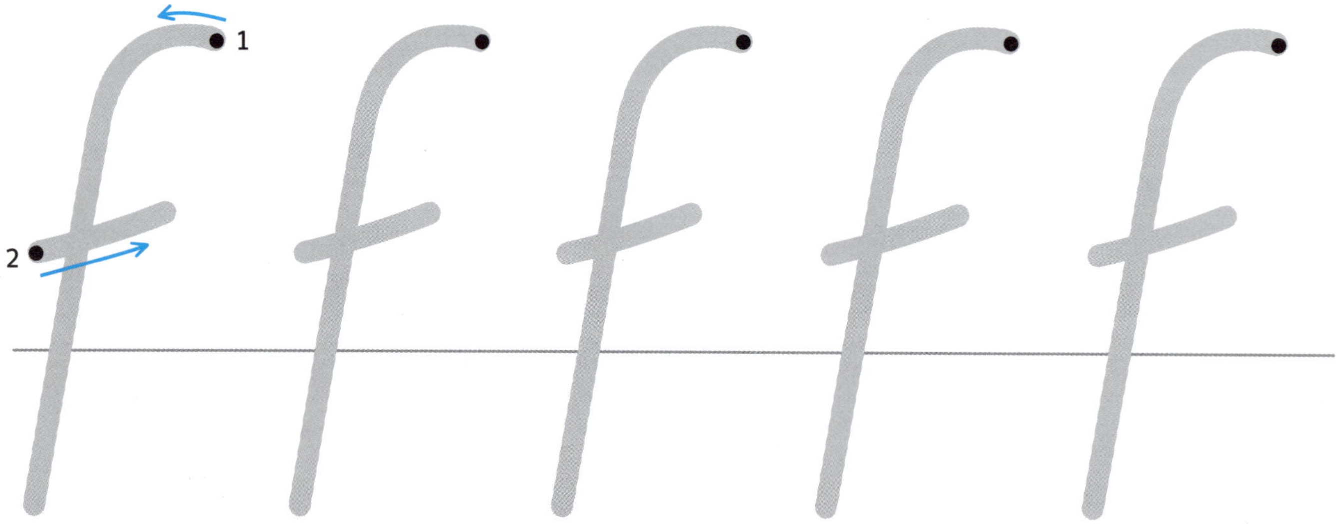

1

2

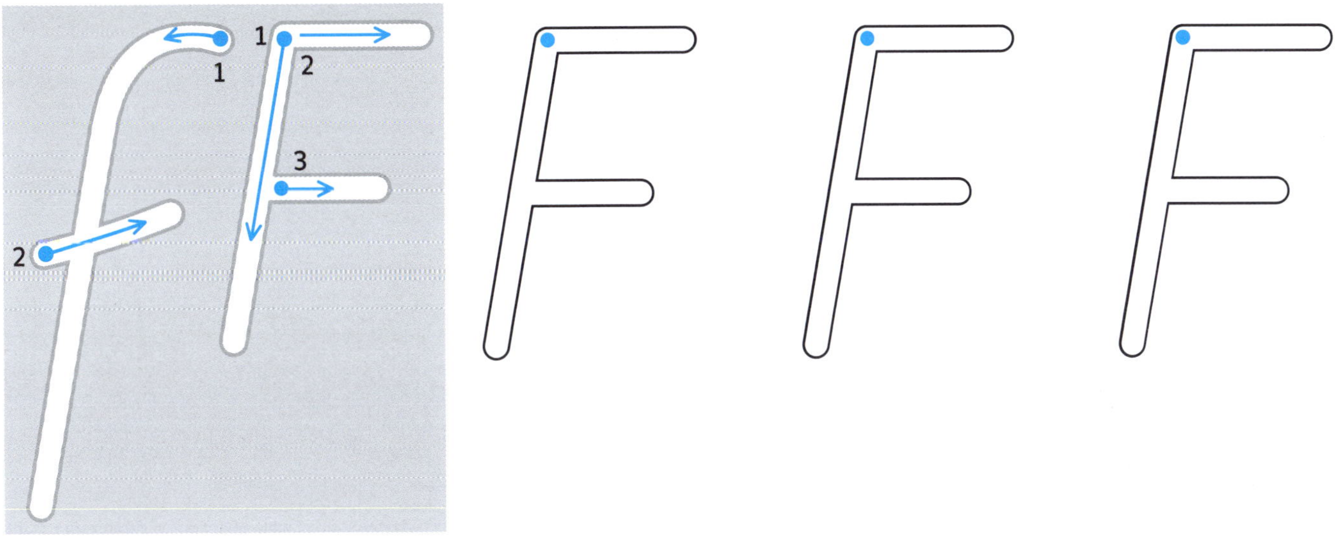

f F

feather

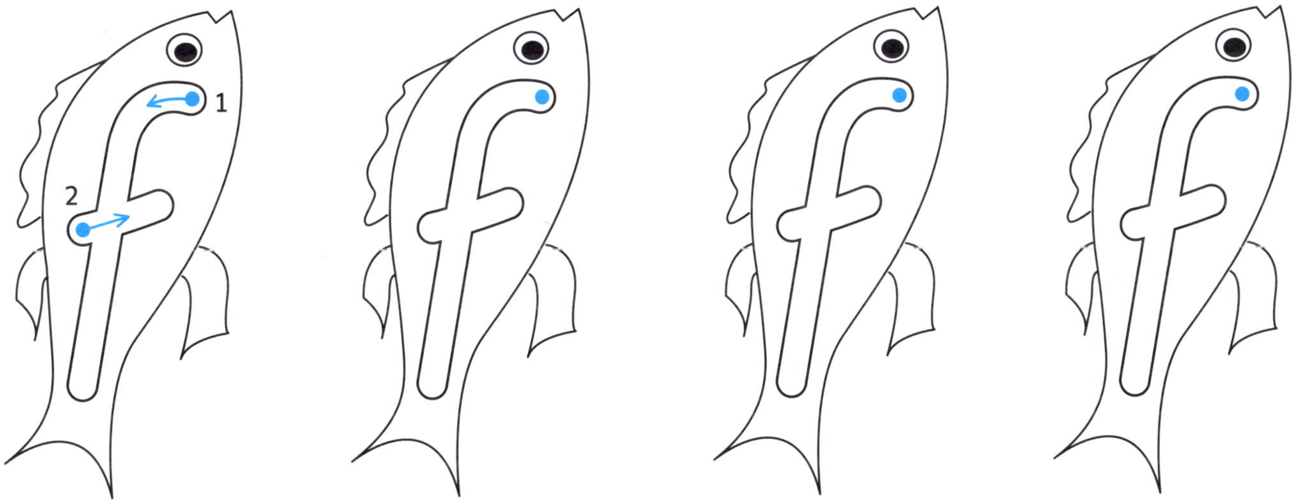

fish

Trace the letter.

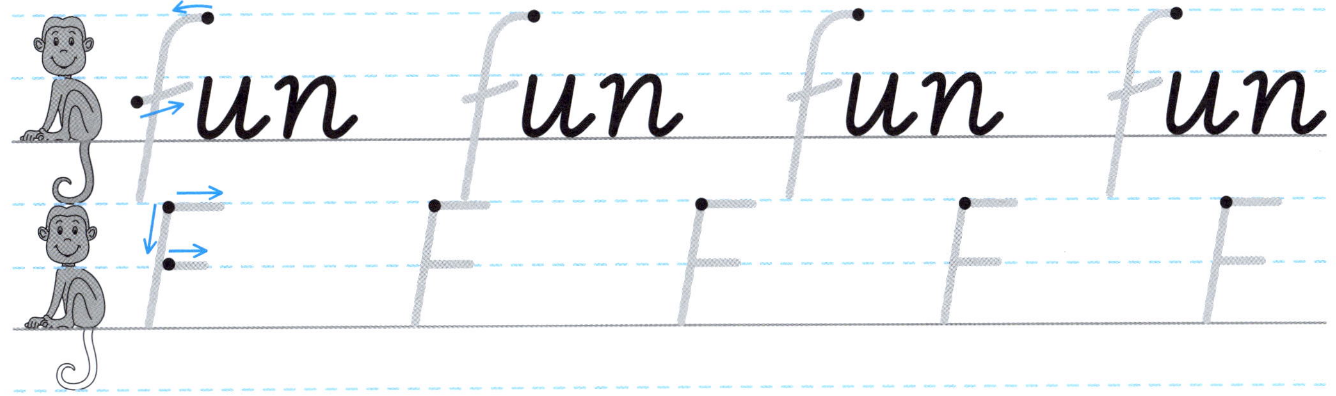

ISBN: 9780170421416

Start at the dot. Follow the arrow.

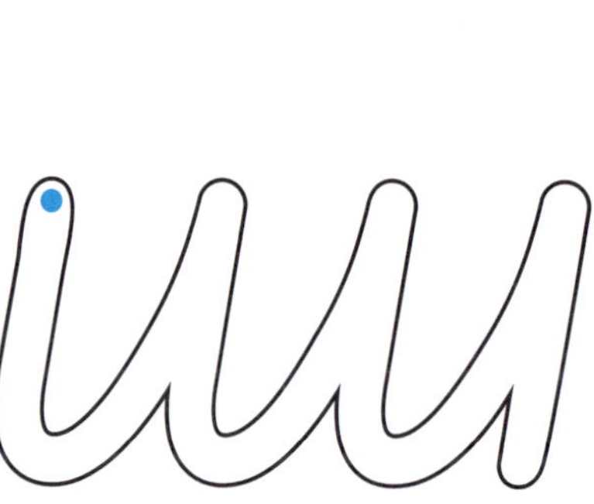

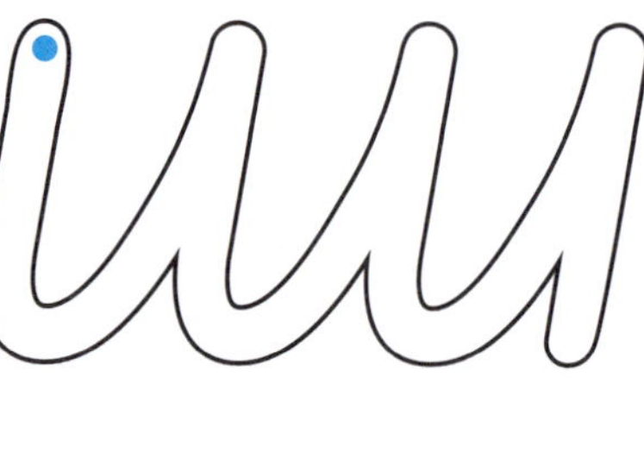

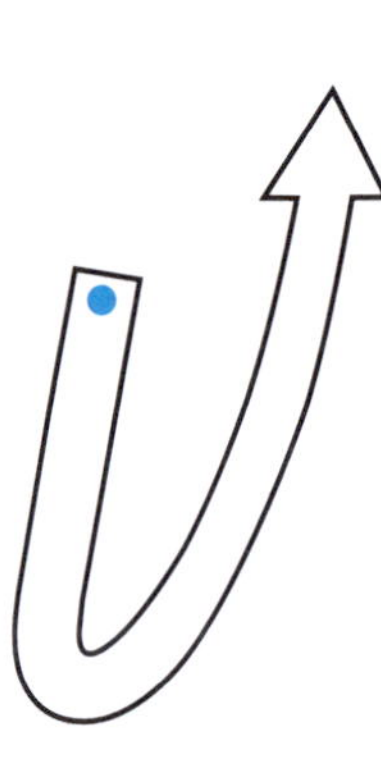

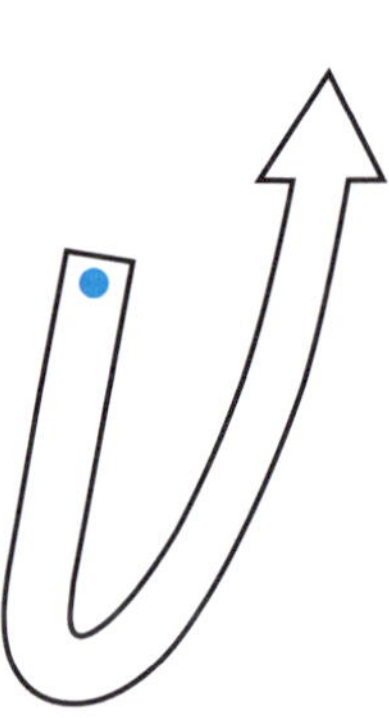

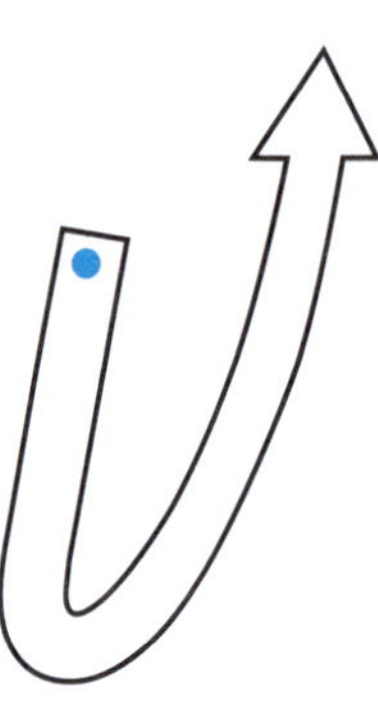

up

ISBN: 9780170421416

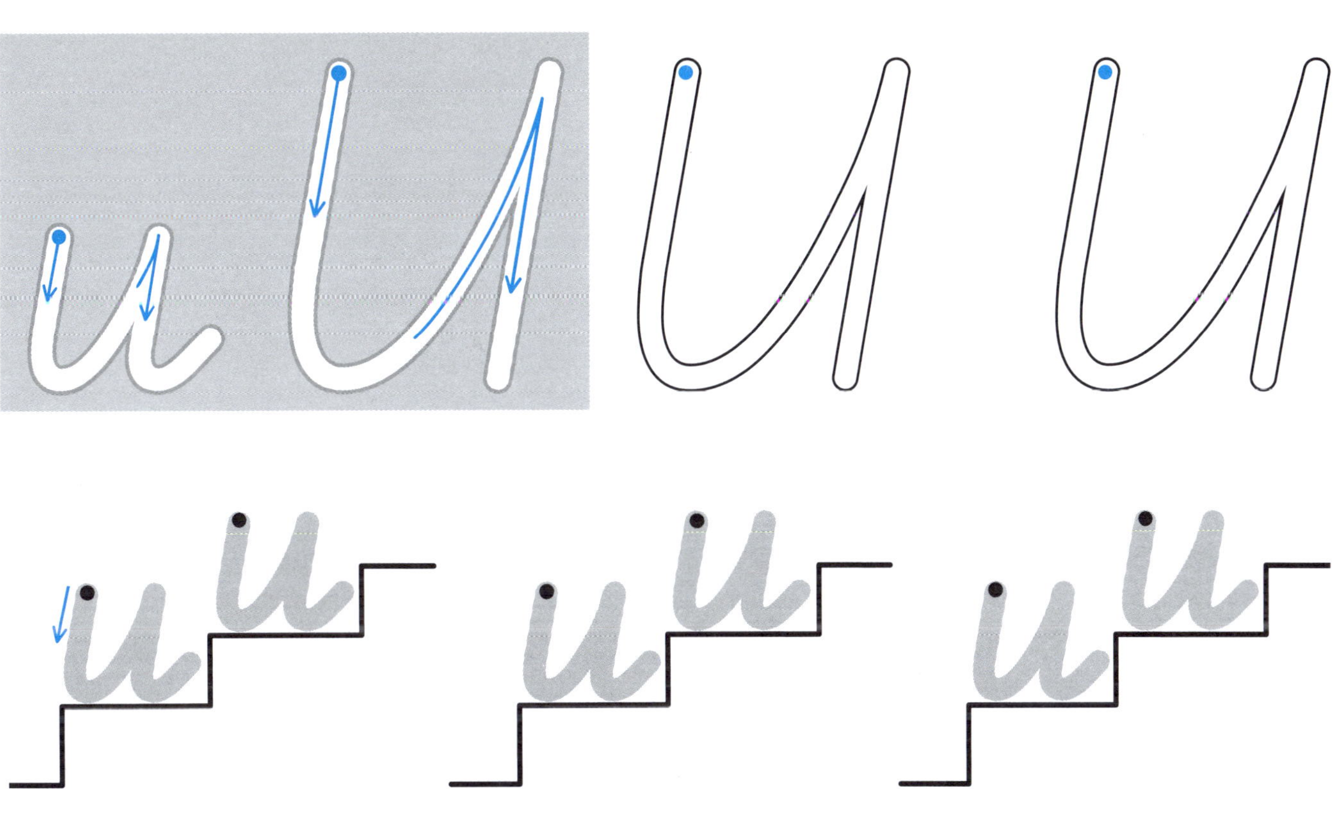

upstairs

umbrella

Trace the letter.

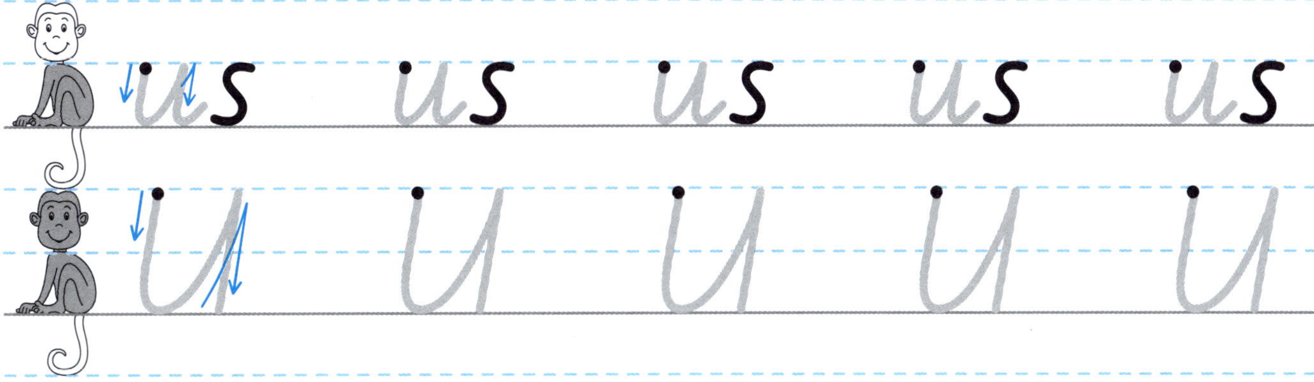

yo-yo

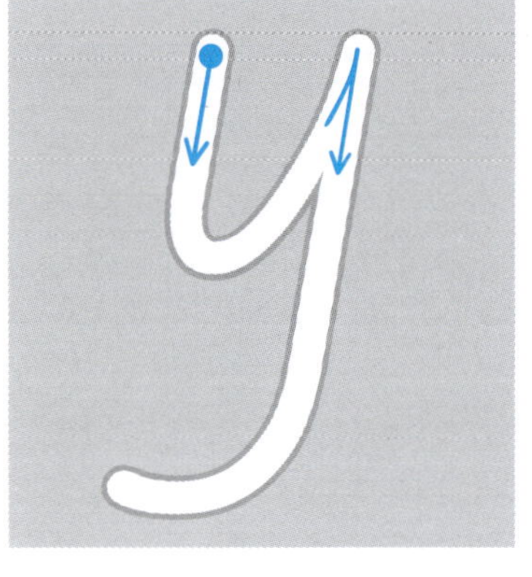

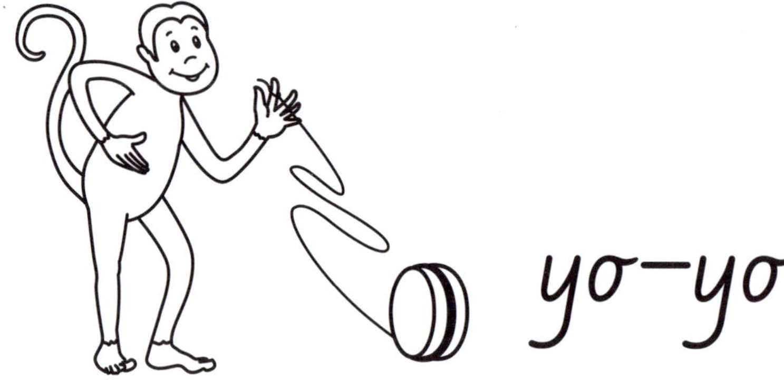

Start at the dot. Follow the arrow.

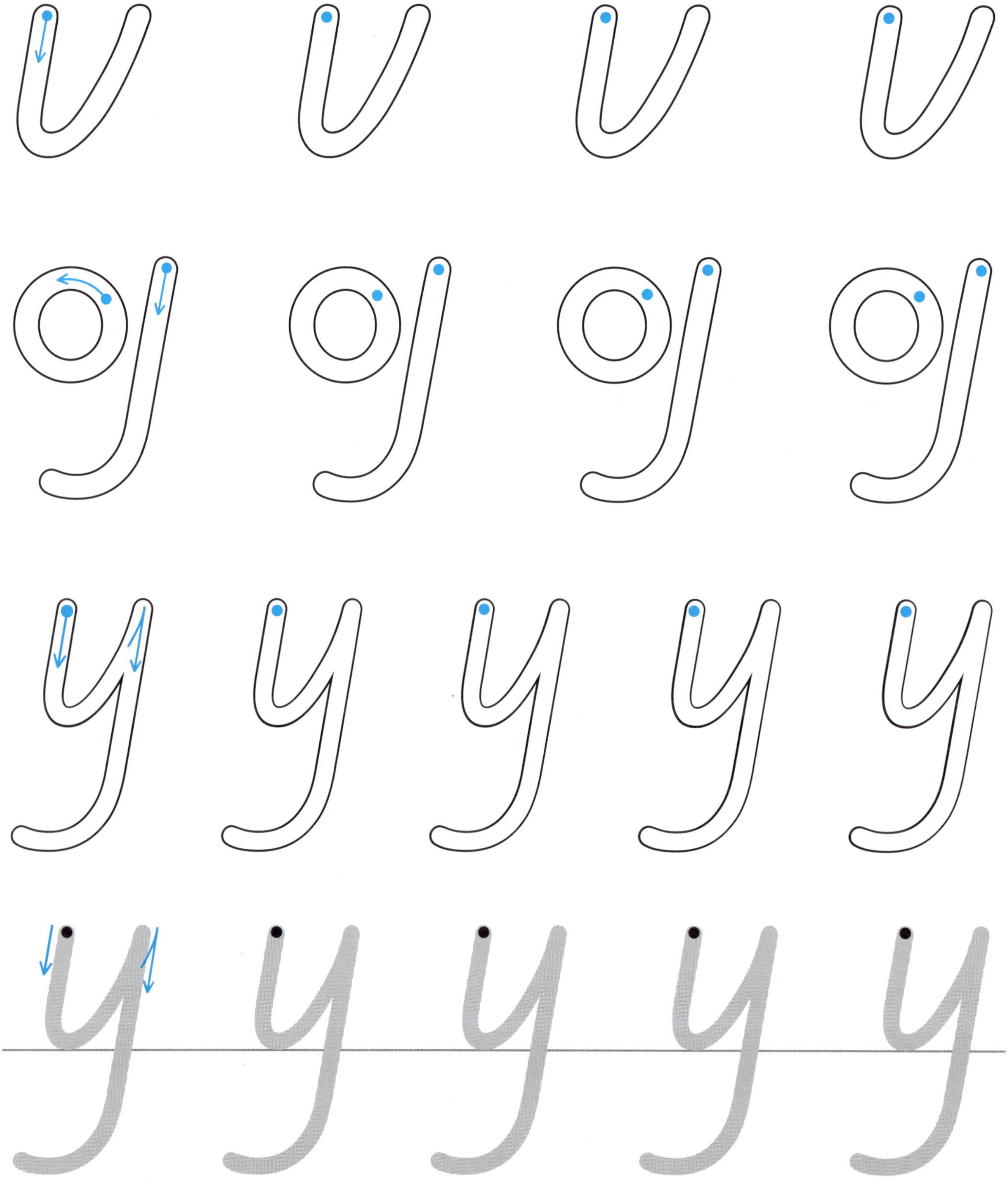

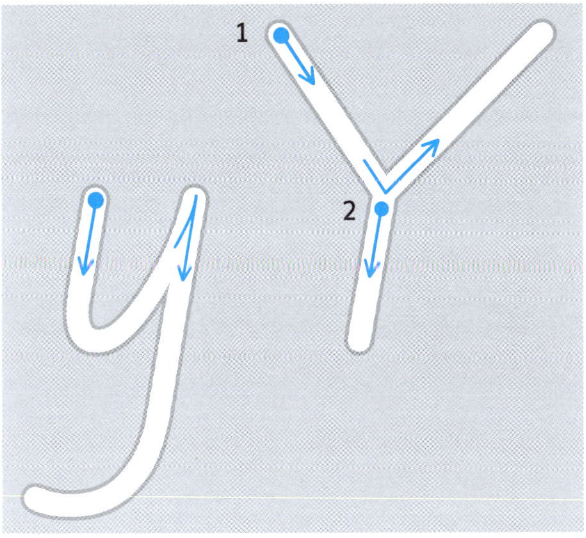

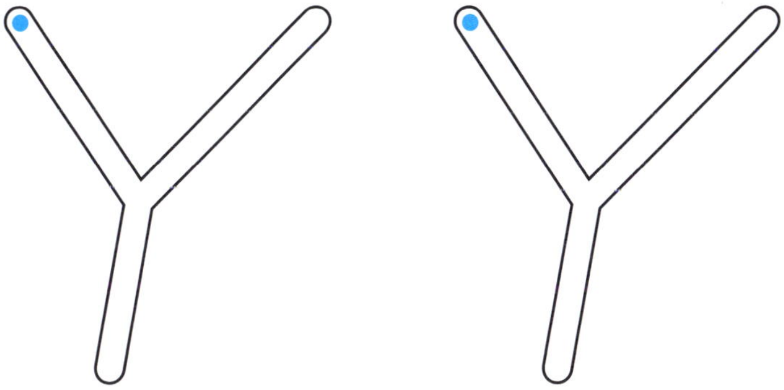

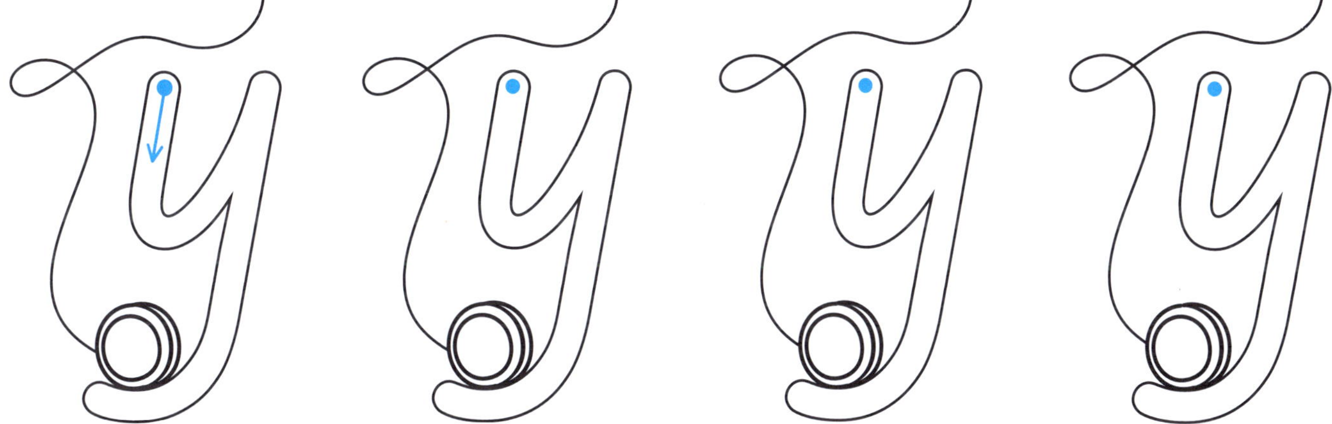

yo-yo

Trace the letter.

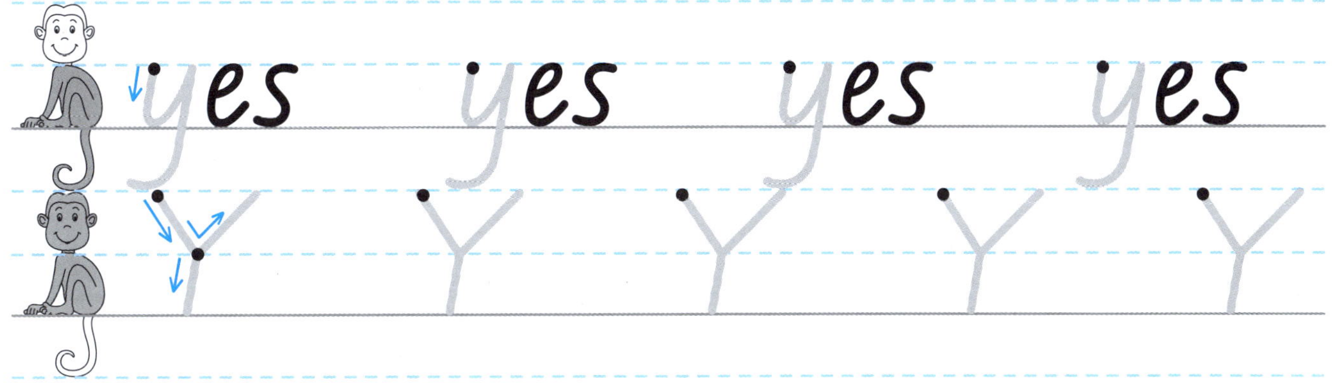

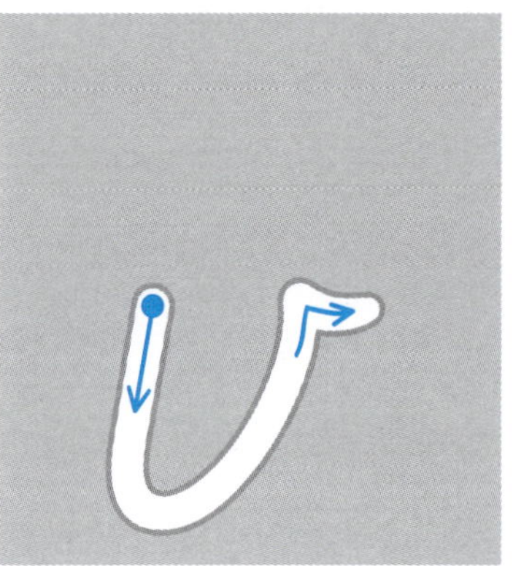

van

Start at the dot. Follow the arrow.

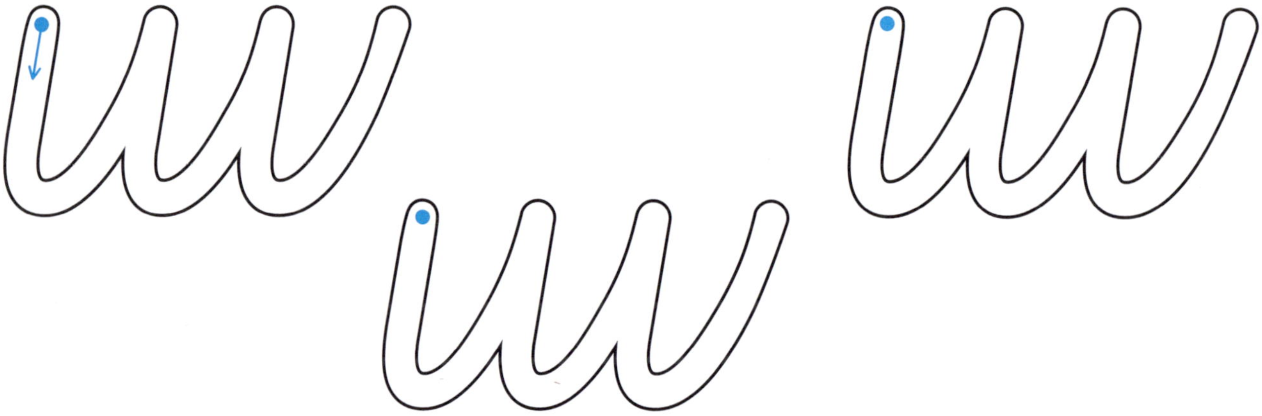

volcano

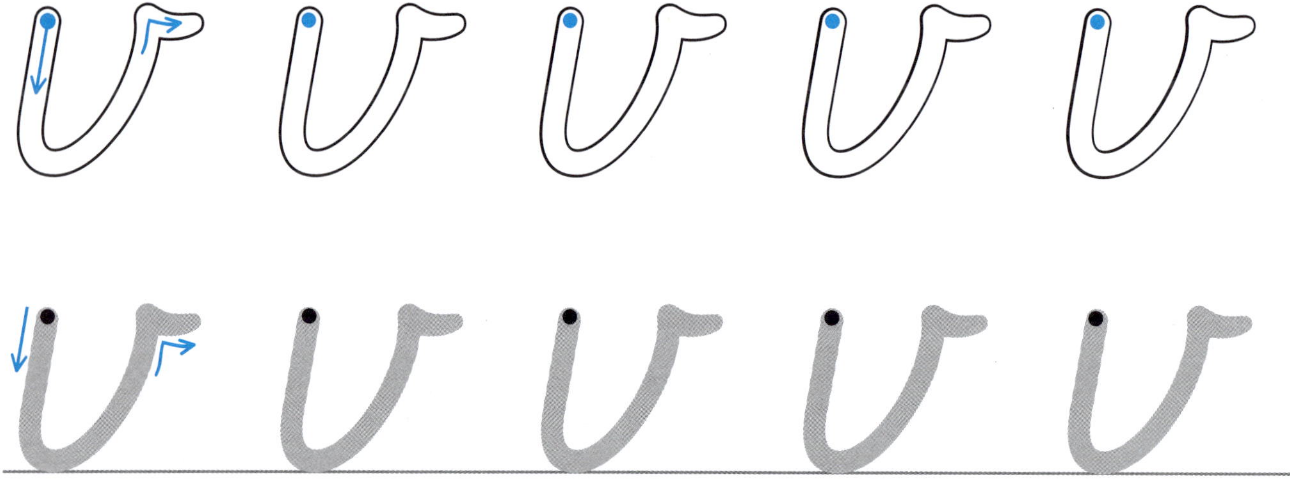

Trace the letter.

window

Start at the dot. Follow the arrow.

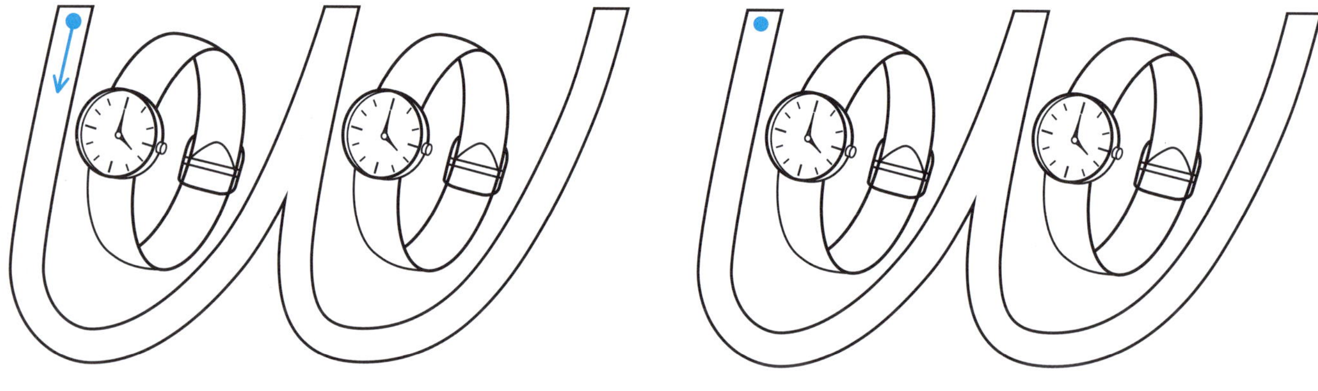

watch

waves

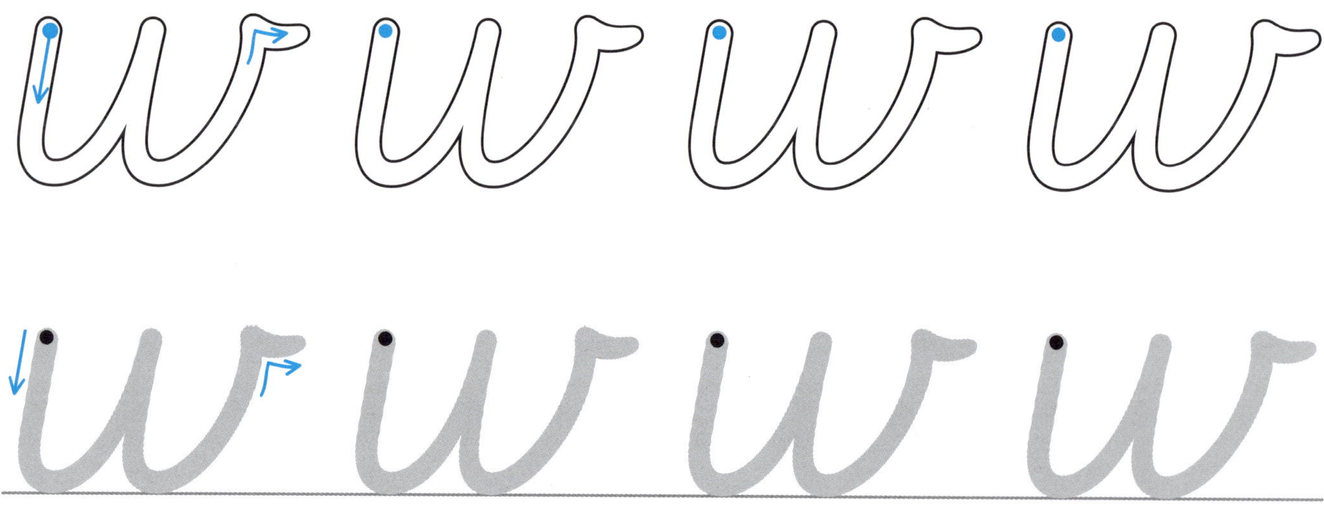

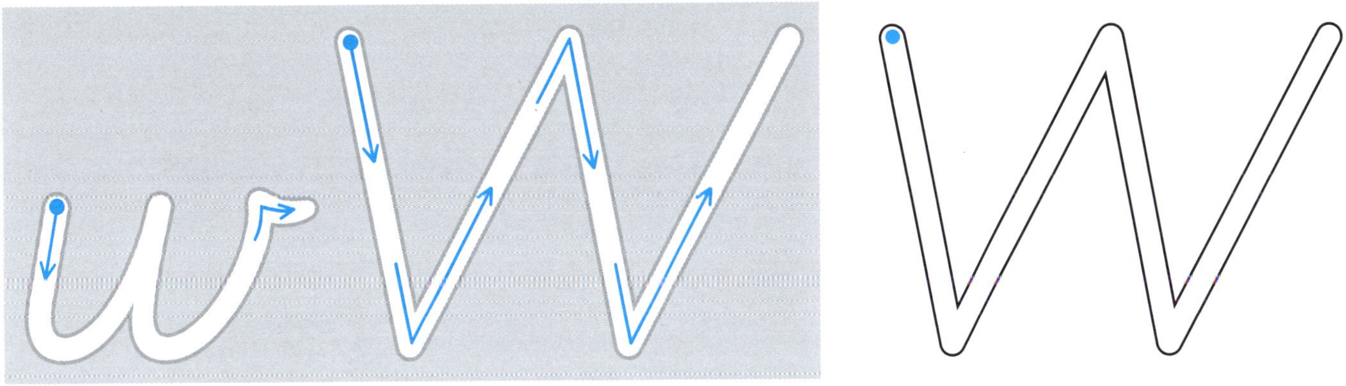

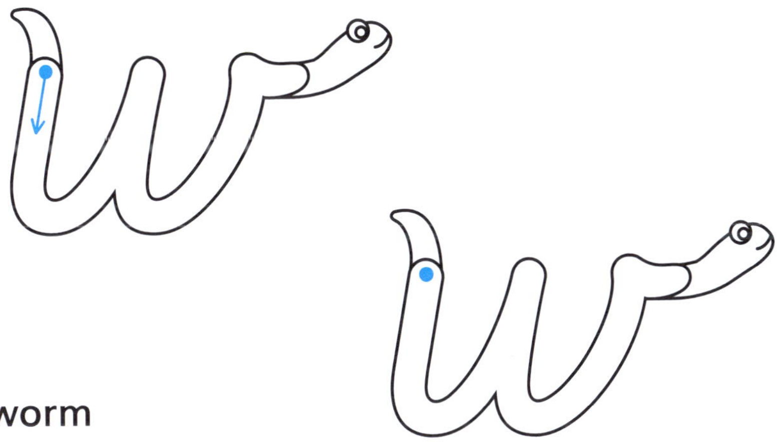

worm

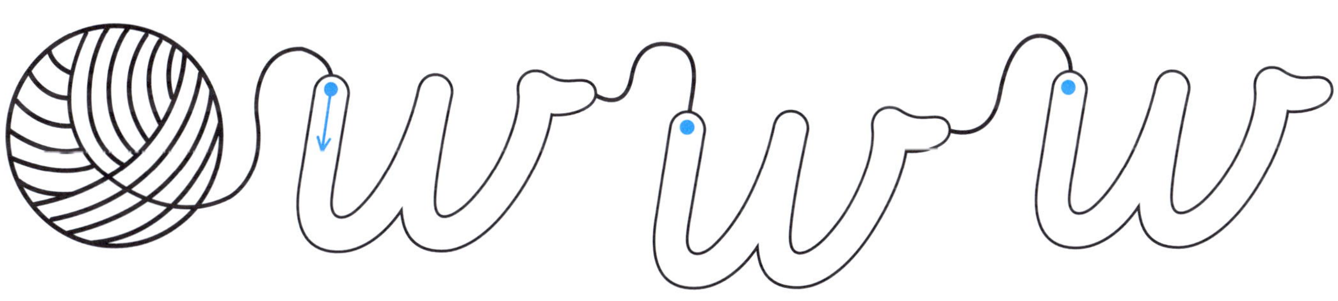

wool

Trace the letter.

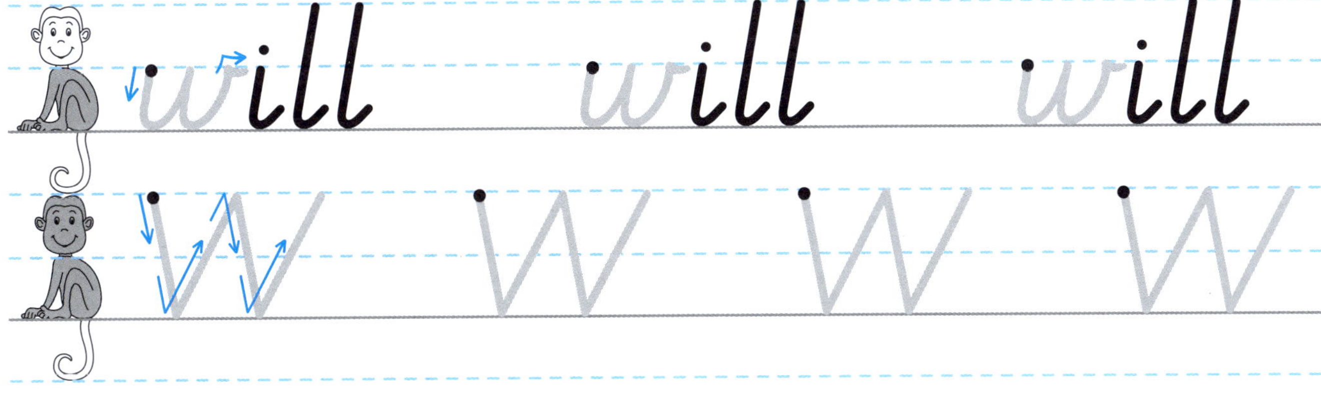

ISBN: 9780170421416

balloons

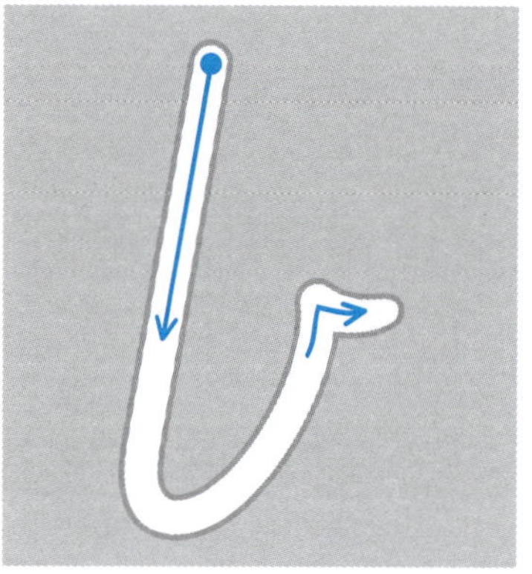

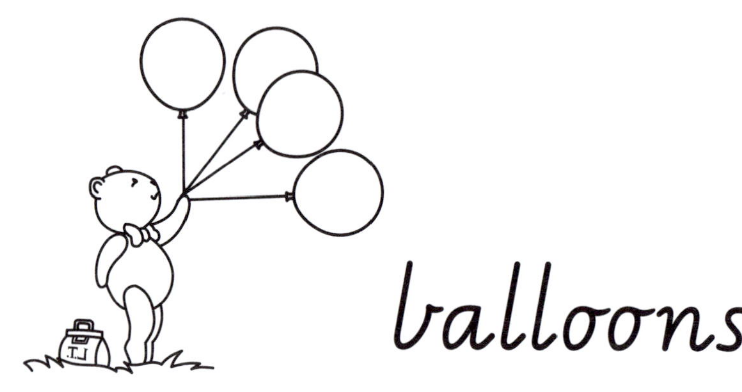

Start at the dot. Follow the arrow.

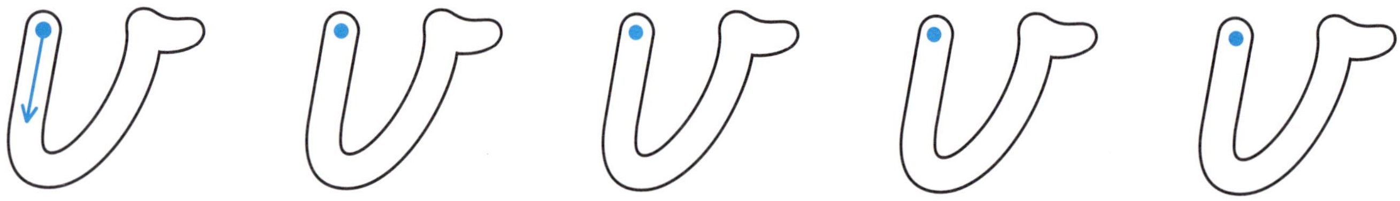

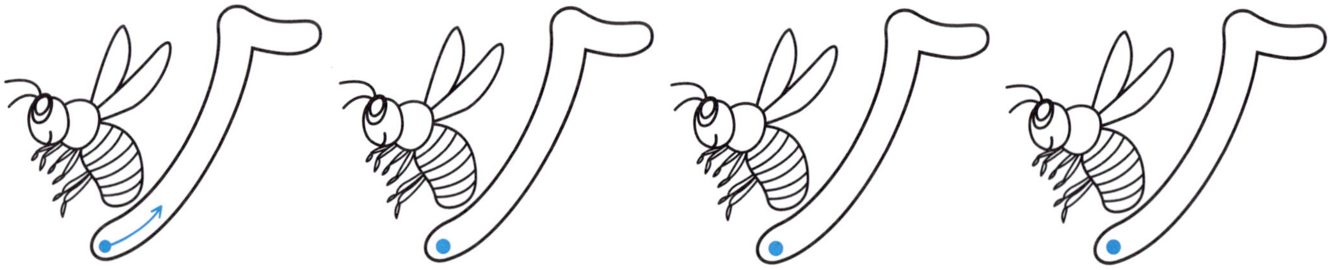

bee

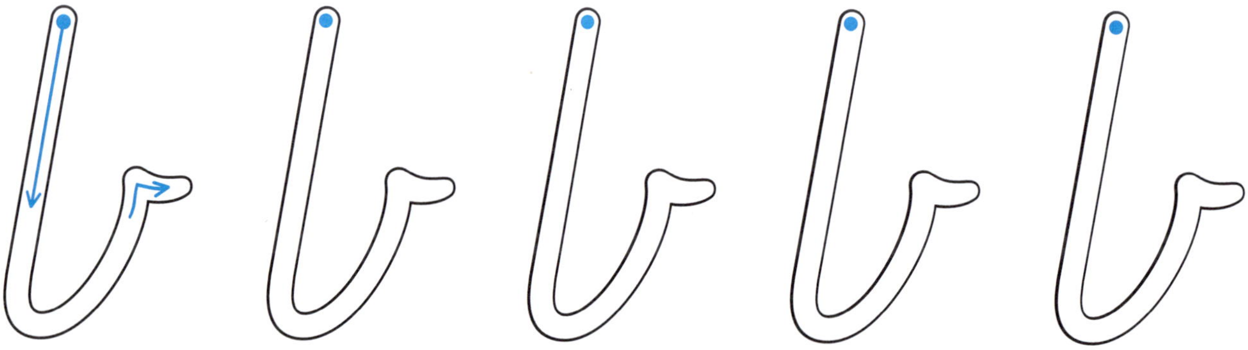

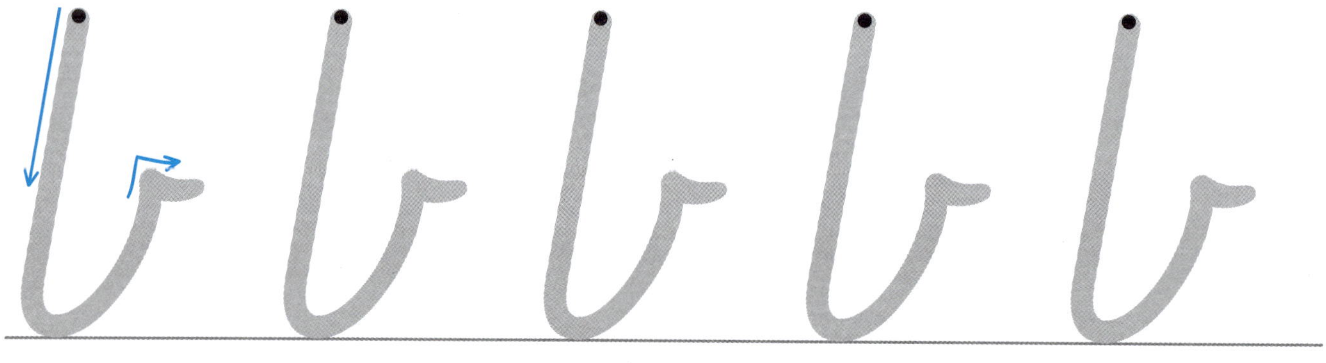

boat

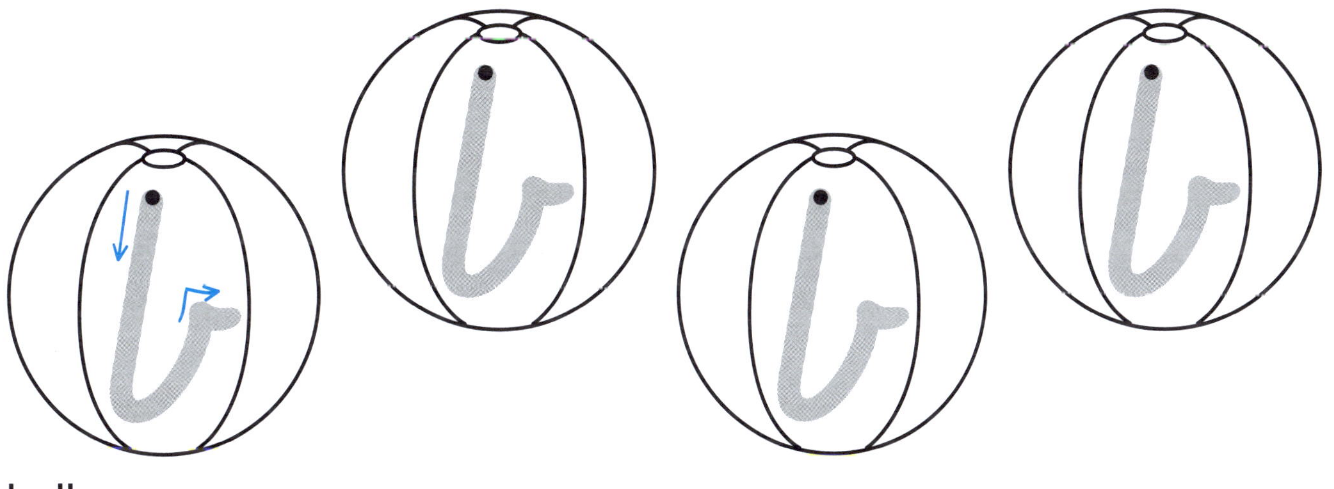

ball

get.ga/PMWA203

Trace the letter.

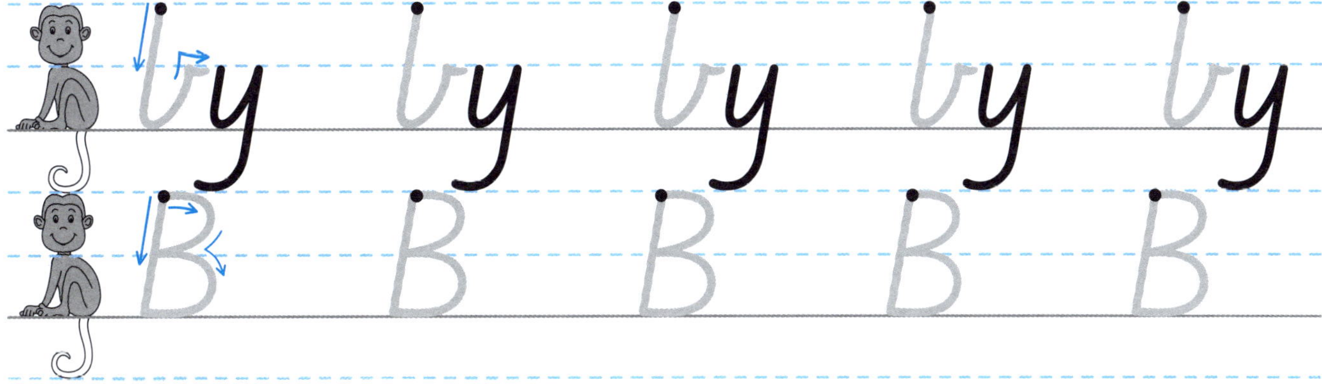

nose

Start at the dot. Follow the arrow.

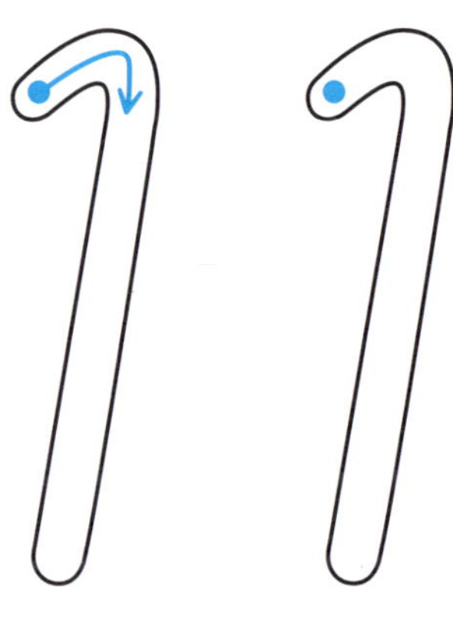

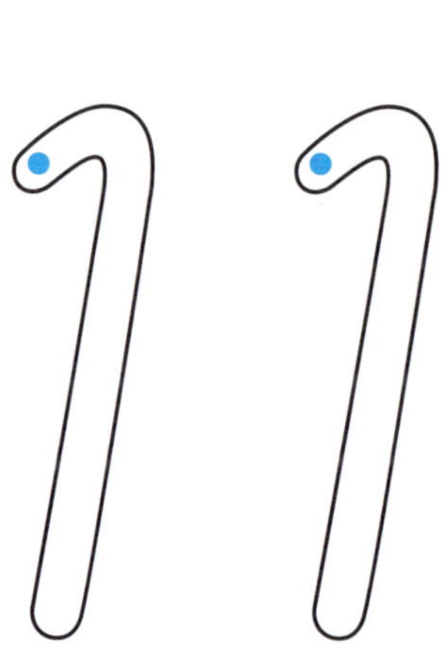

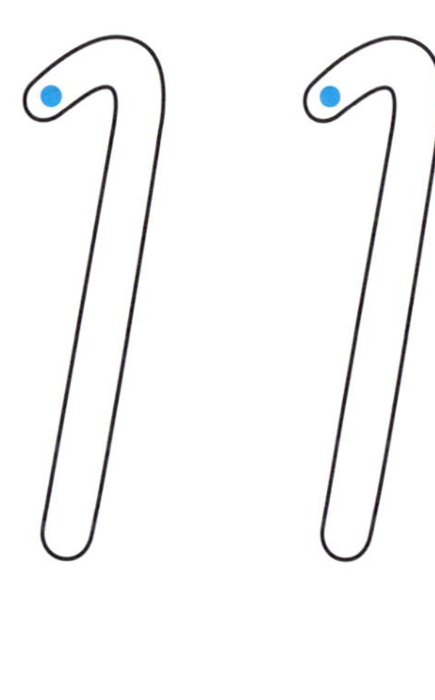

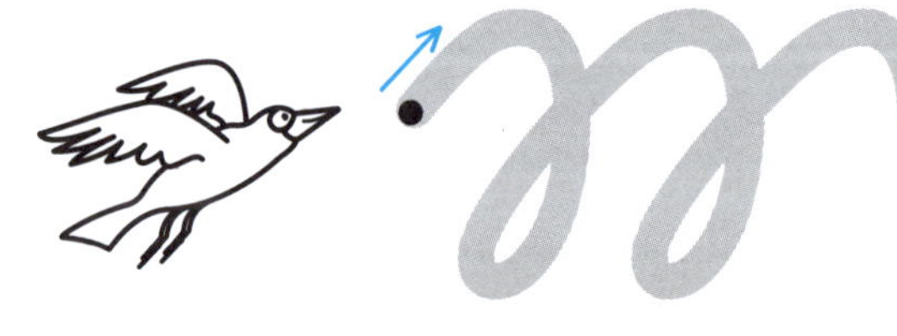

nest

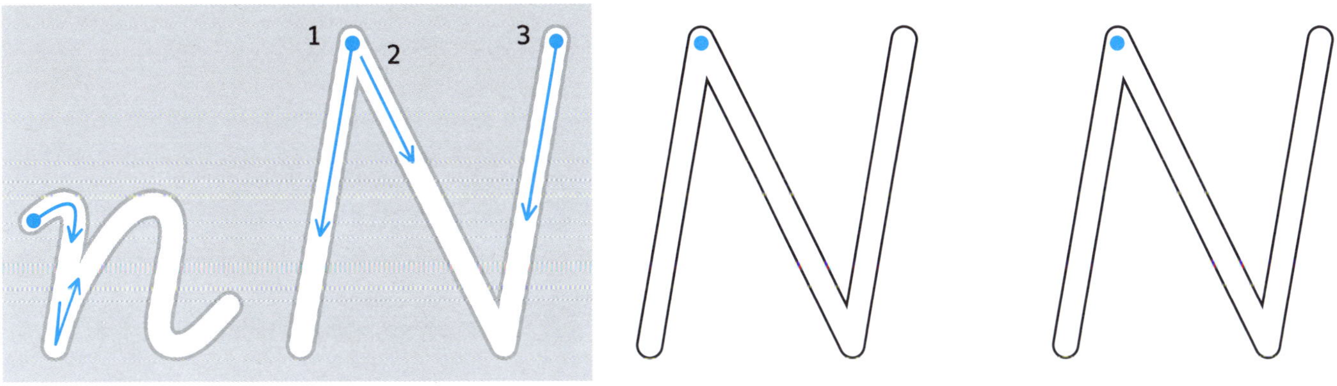

necklace

Trace the letter.

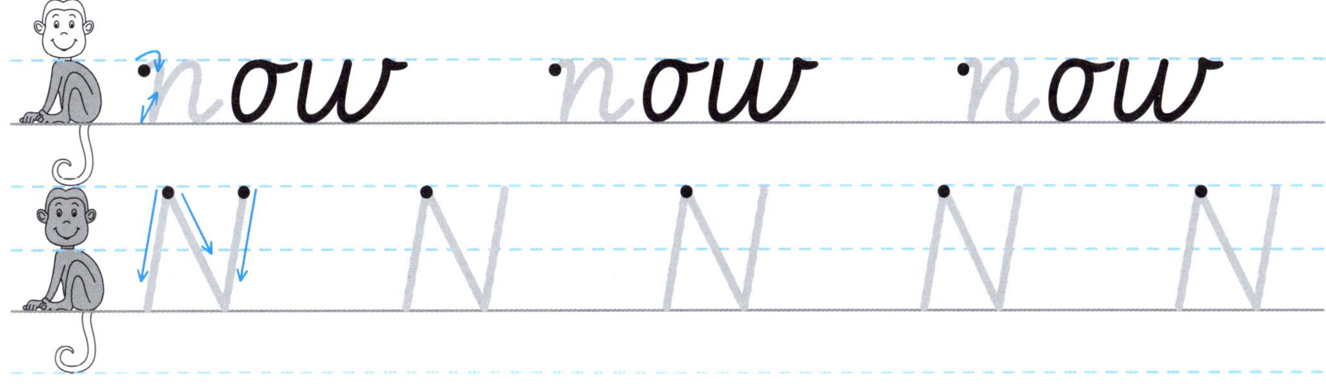

mouse

Start at the dot. Follow the arrow.

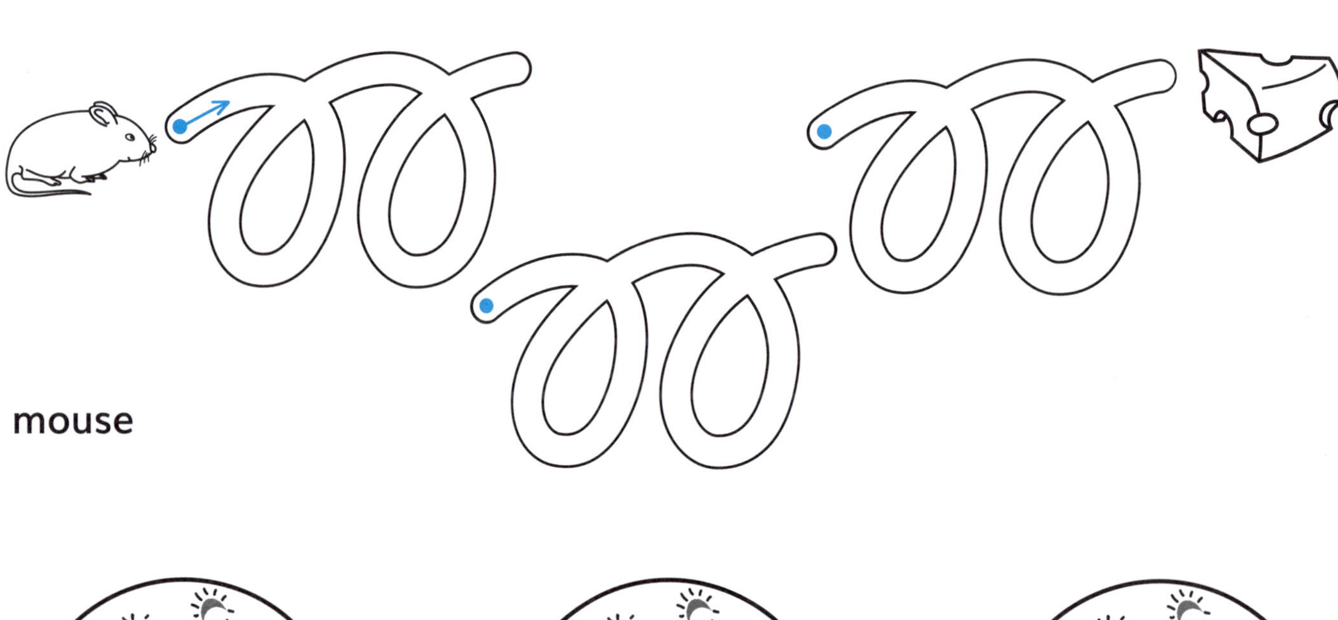

mouse

moon

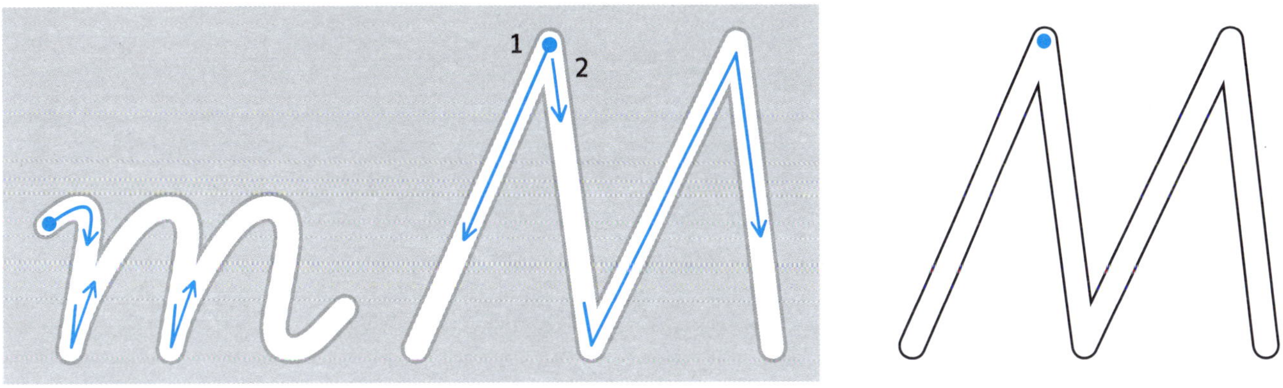

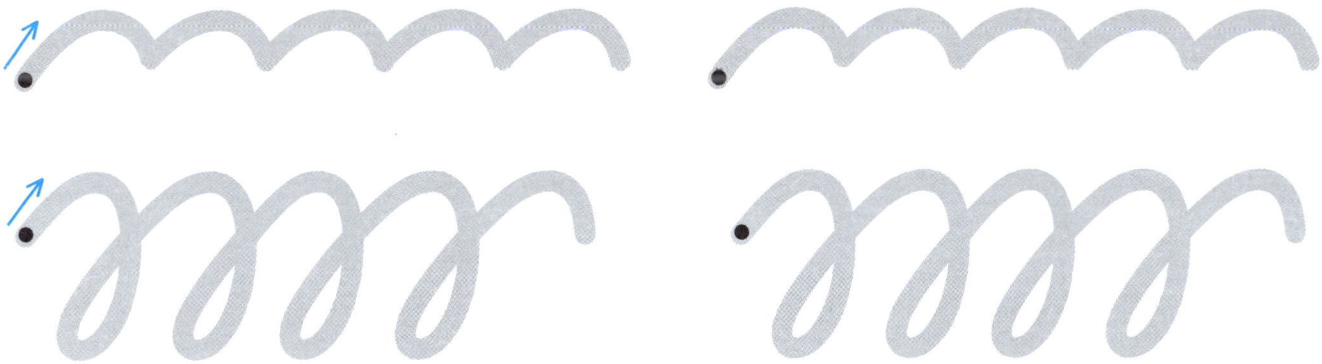

m M

1 2

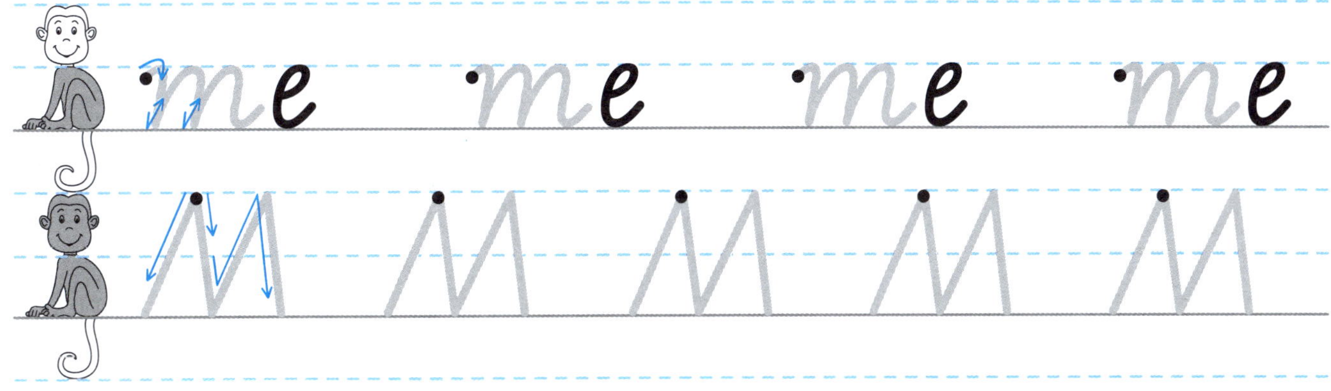

mountains

Trace the letter.

me me me me

M M M M M

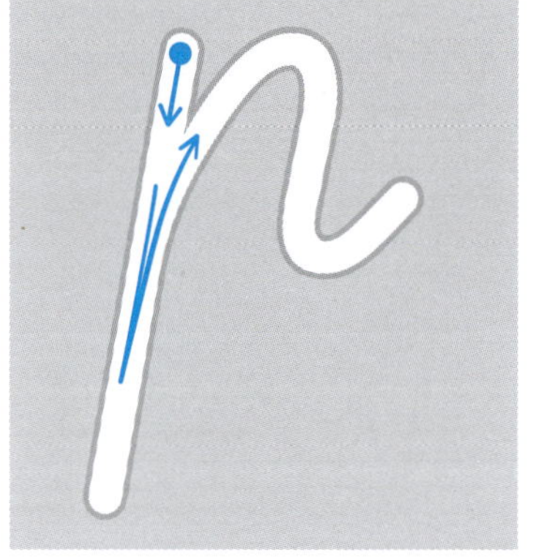

paint

Start at the dot. Follow the arrow.

pencil

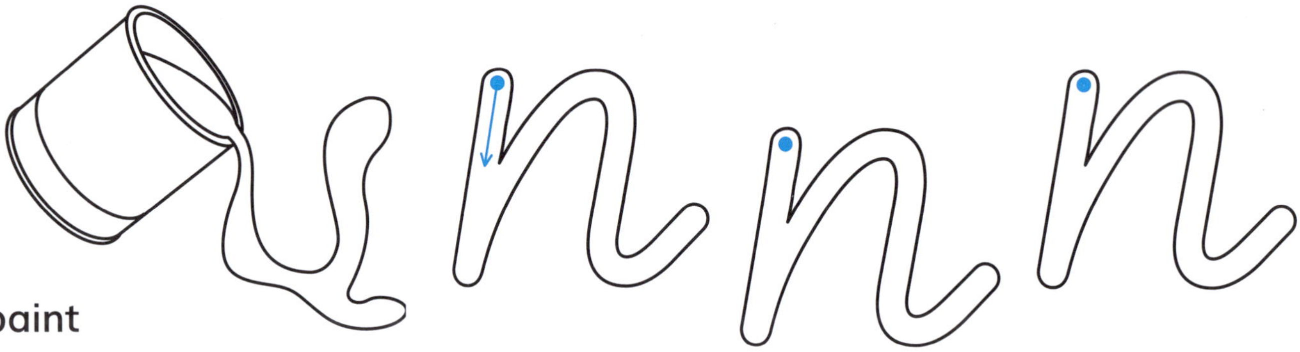

paint

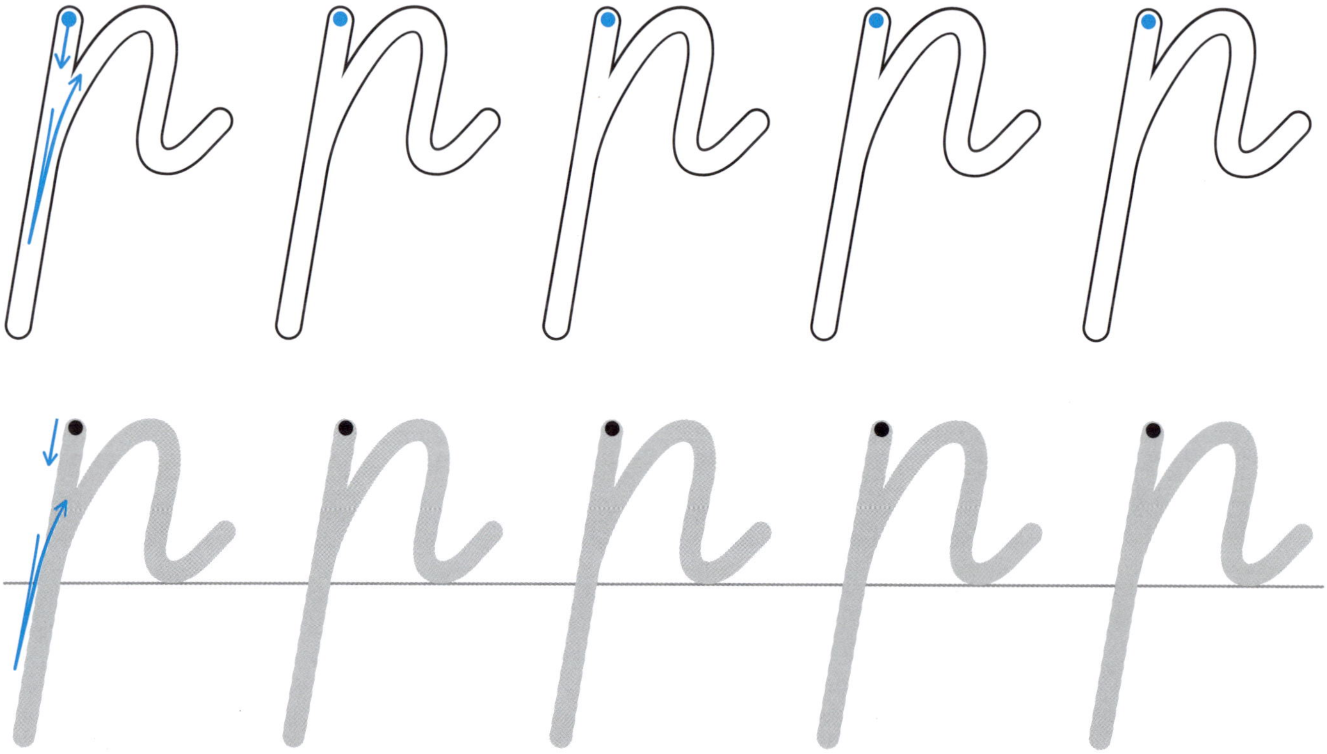

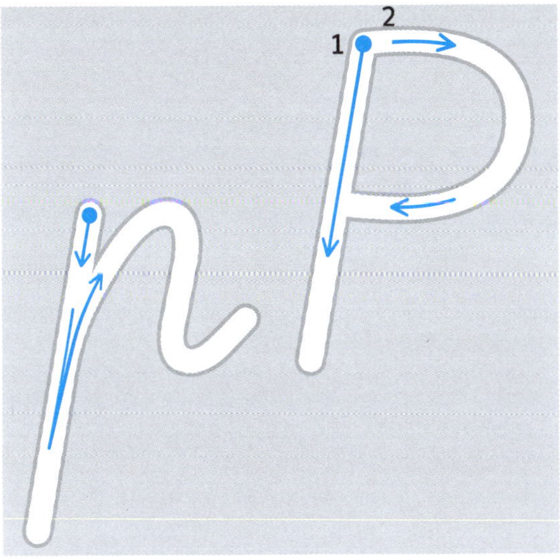

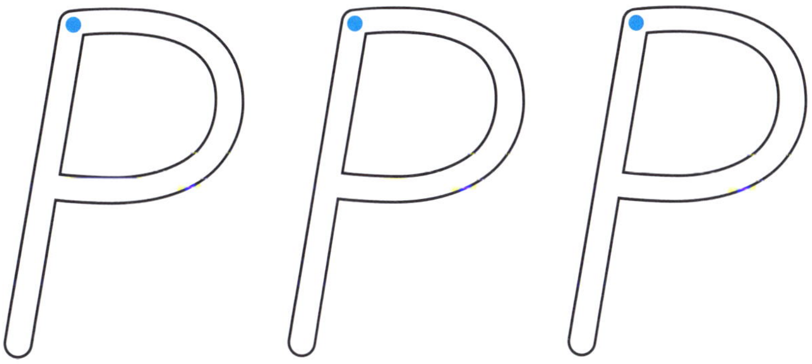

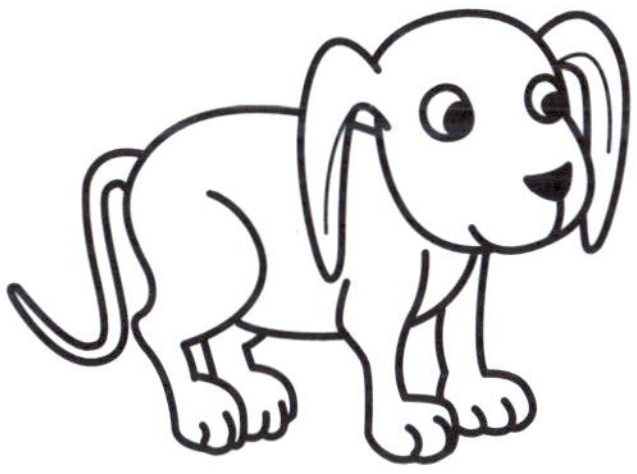

puppy

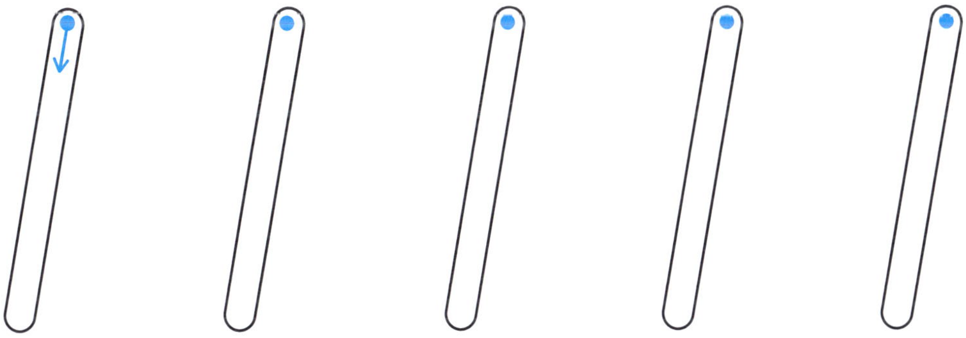

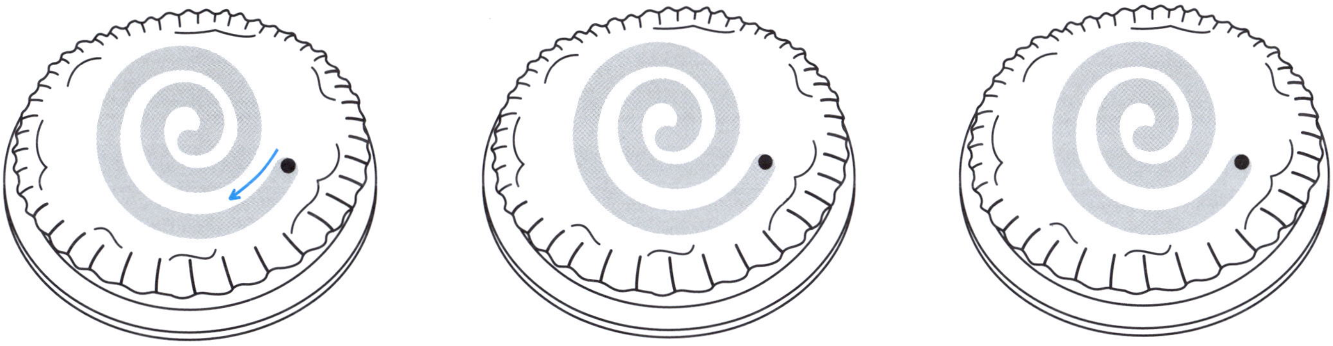

pie

Trace the letter.

play play play

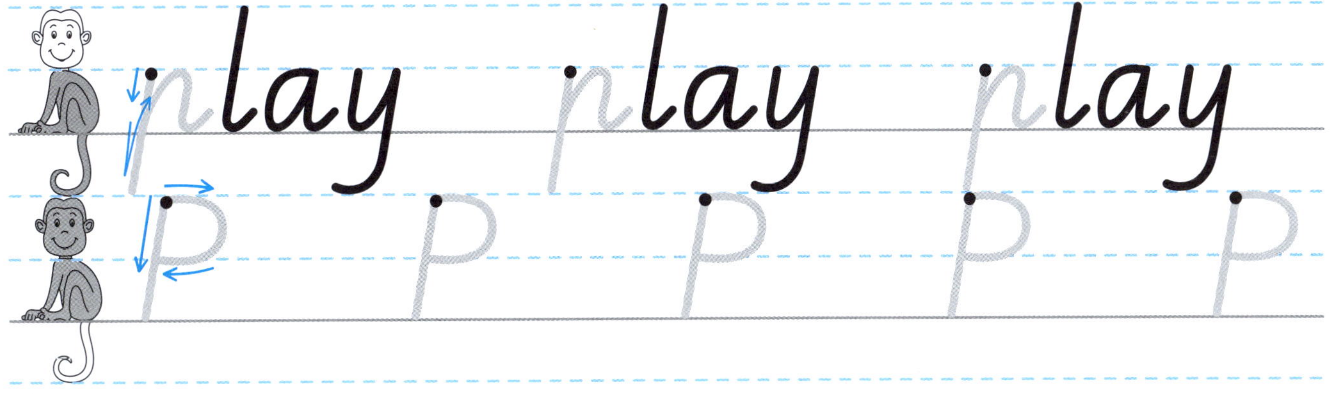

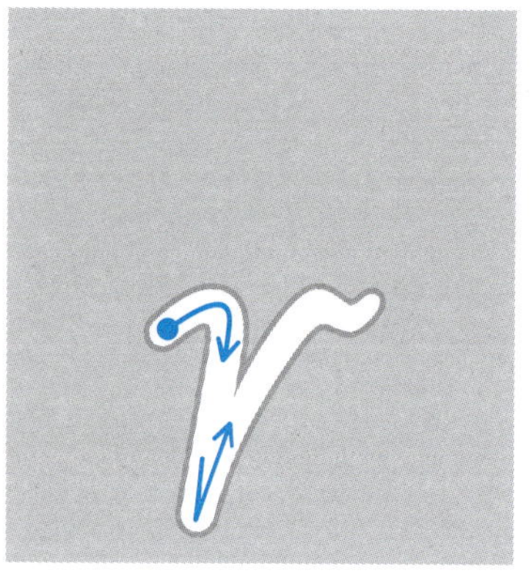

rain

Start at the dot. Follow the arrow.

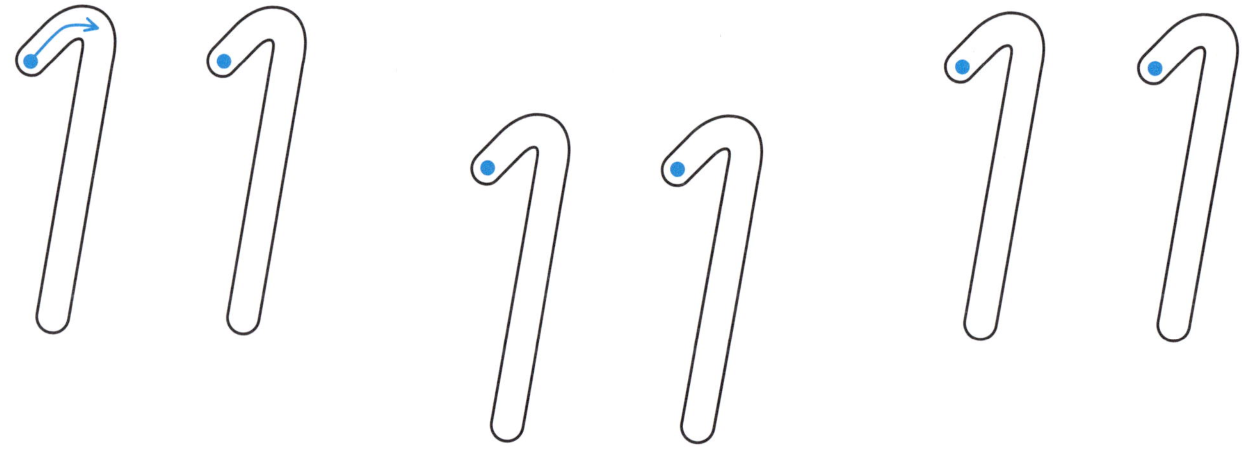

rope

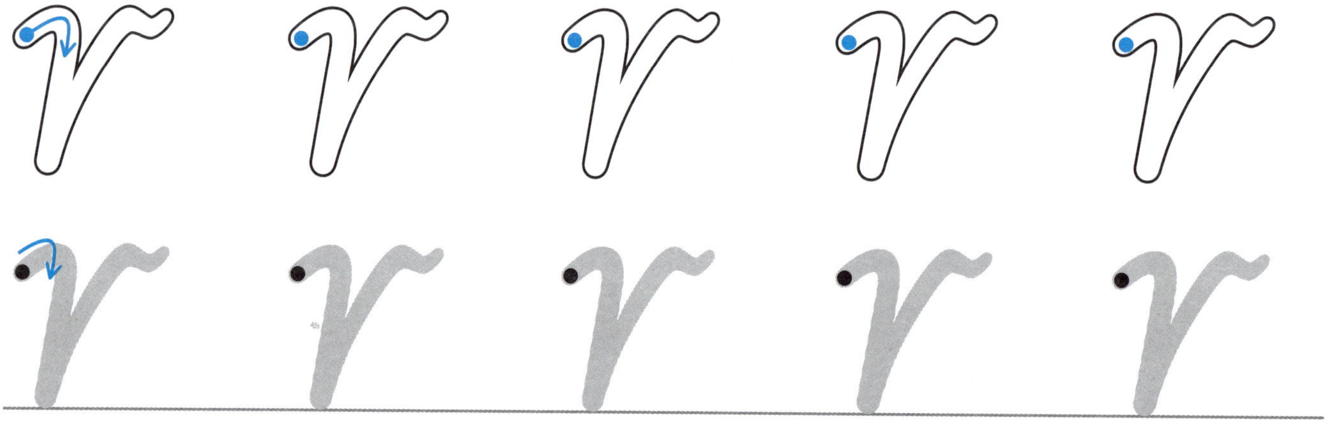

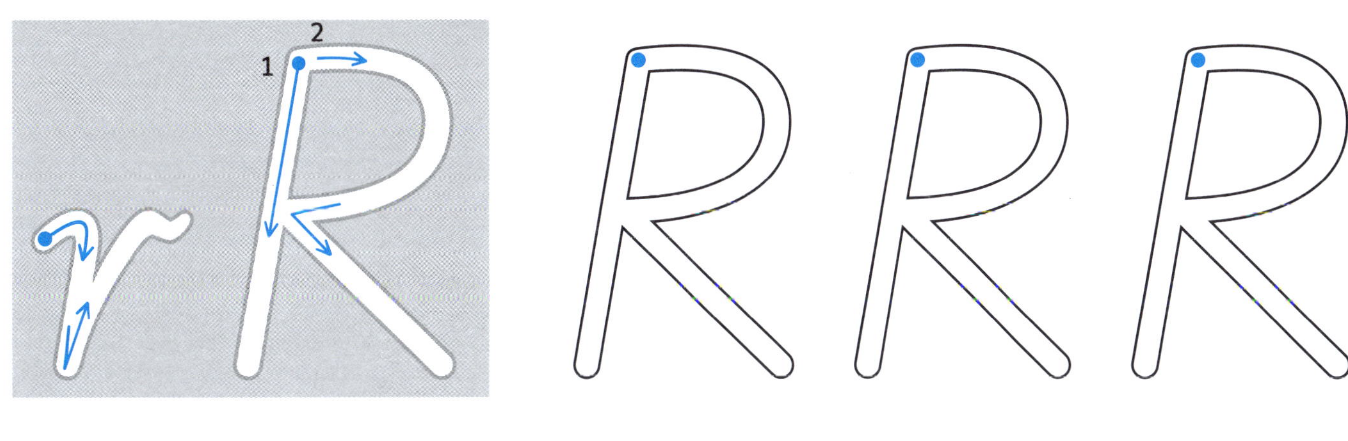

robot

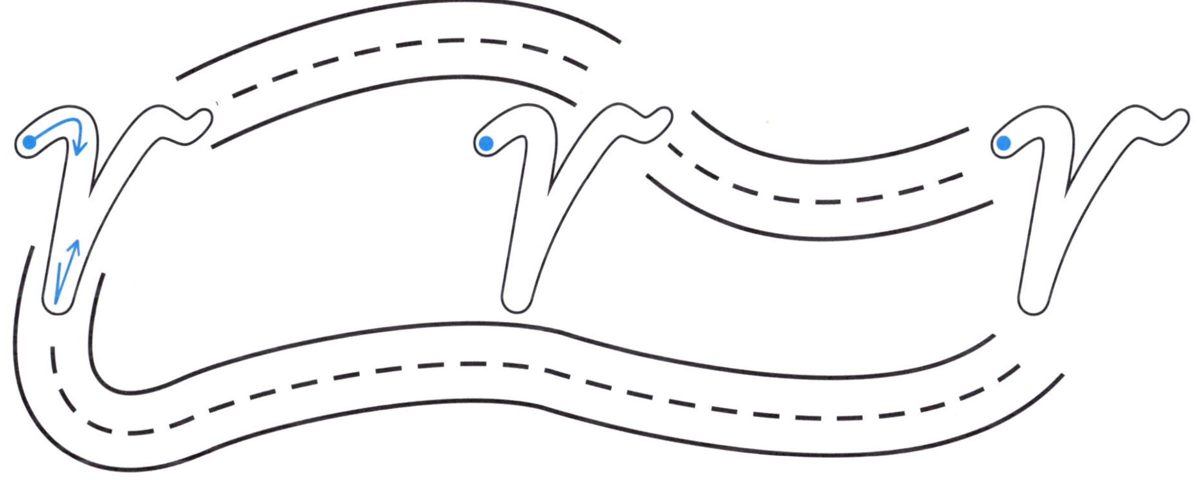

road

Trace the letter.

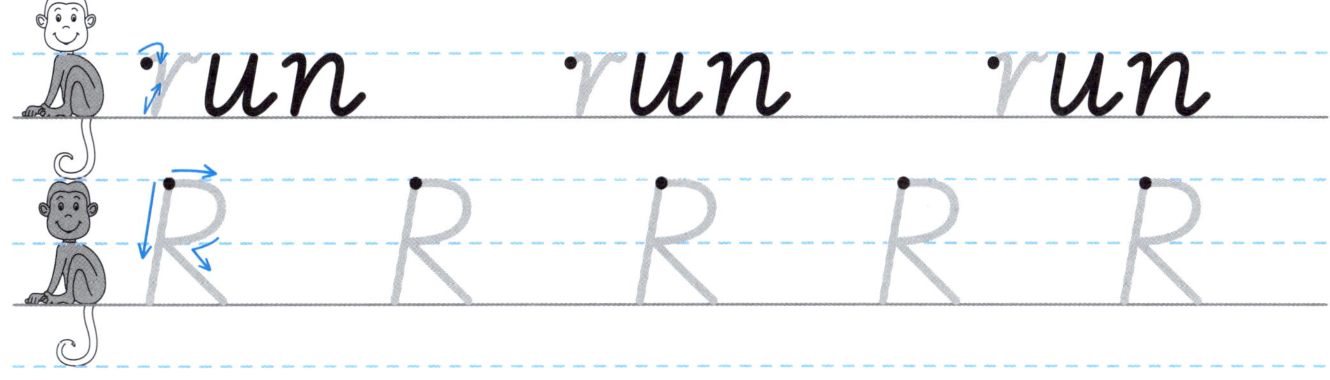

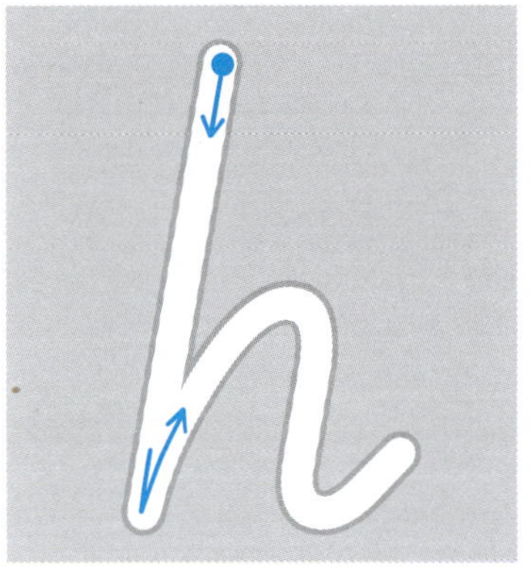

house

Start at the dot. Follow the arrow.

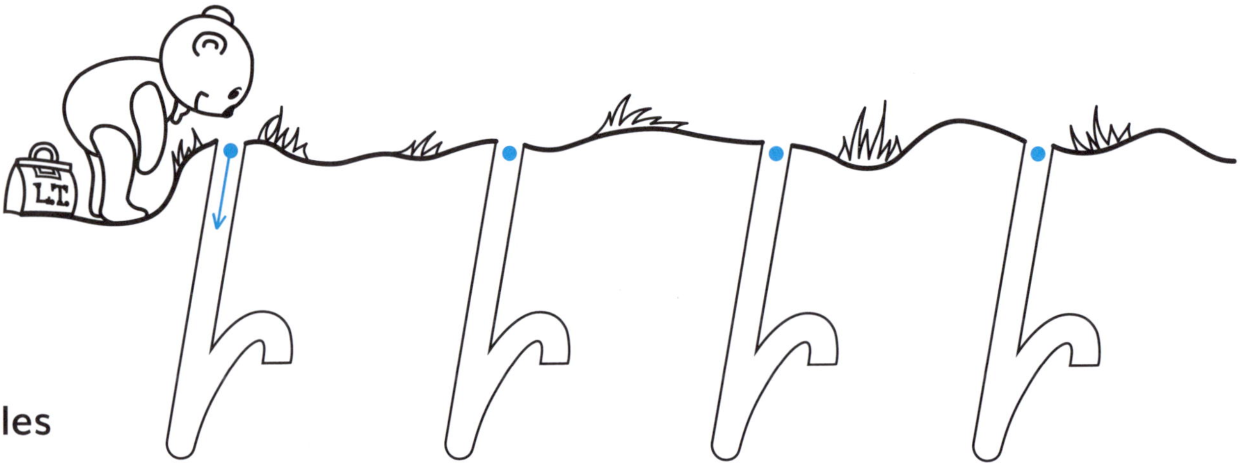

holes

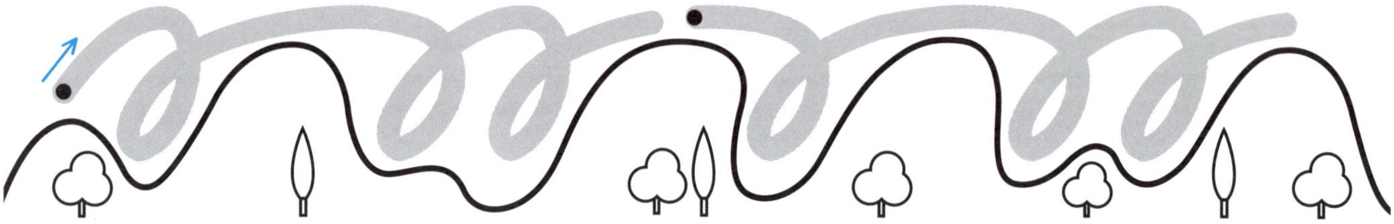

hills

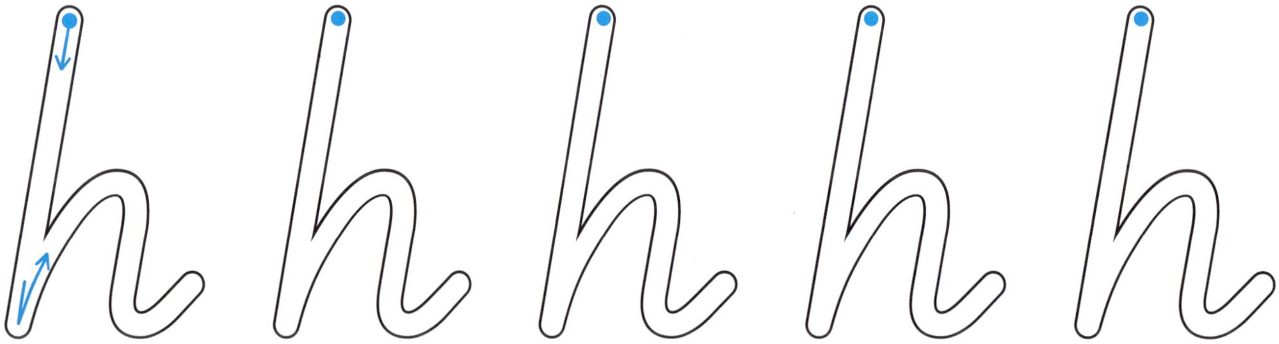

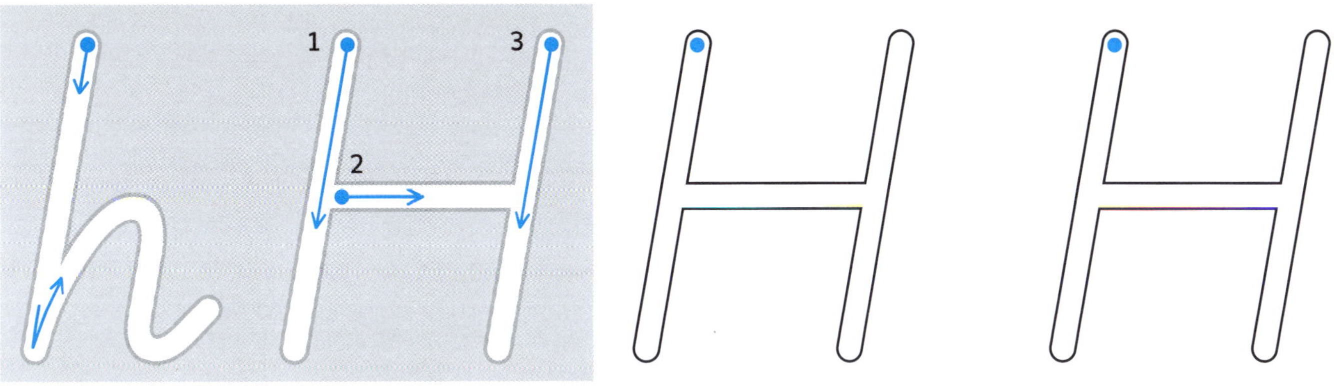

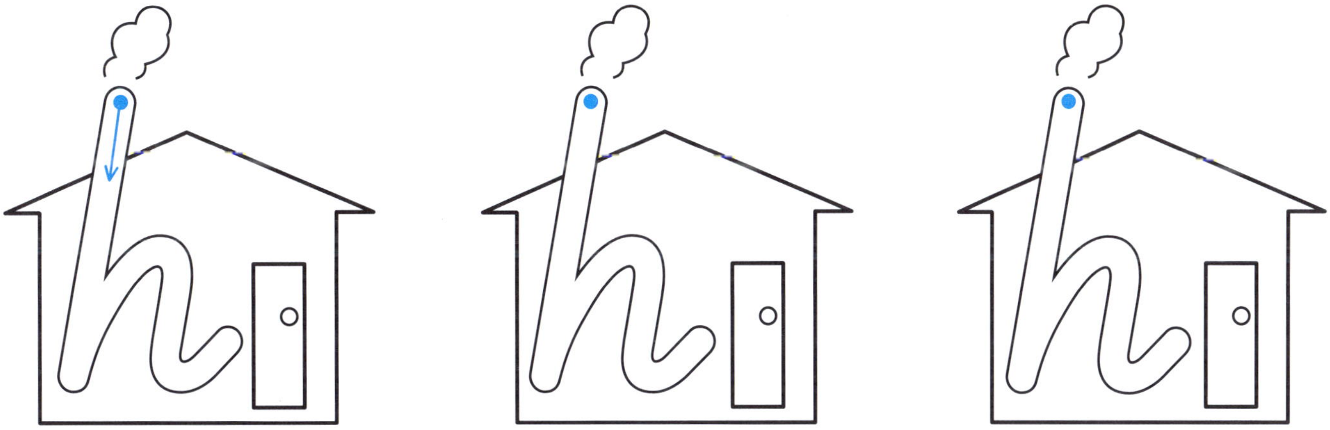

h H H H

house

hat

Trace the letter.

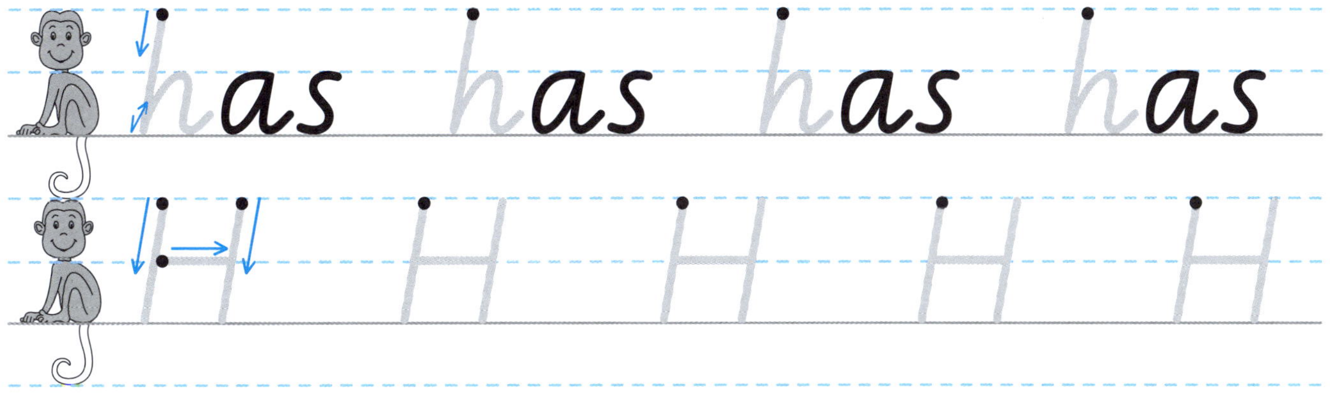

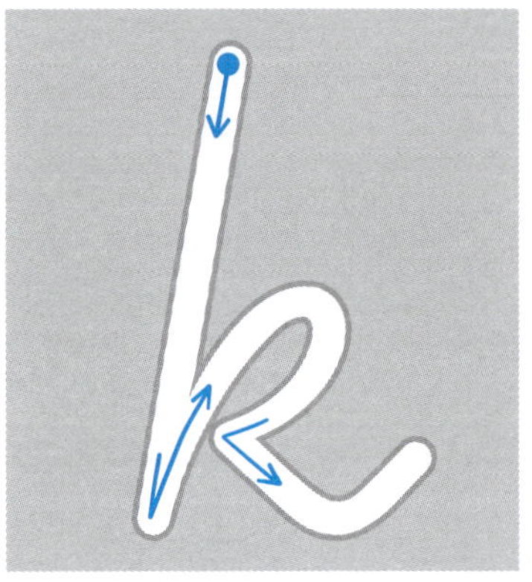

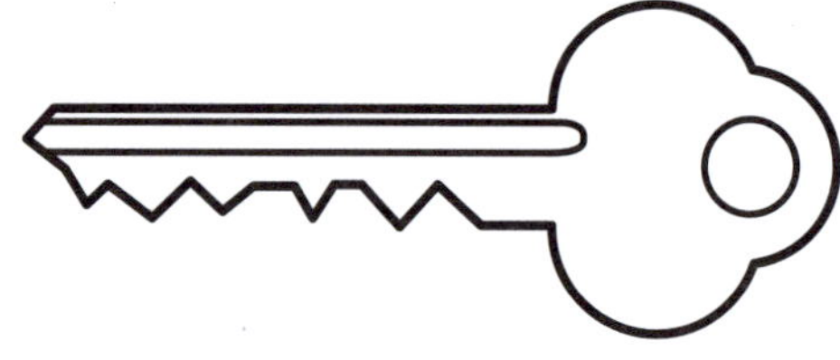

key

Start at the dot. Follow the arrow.

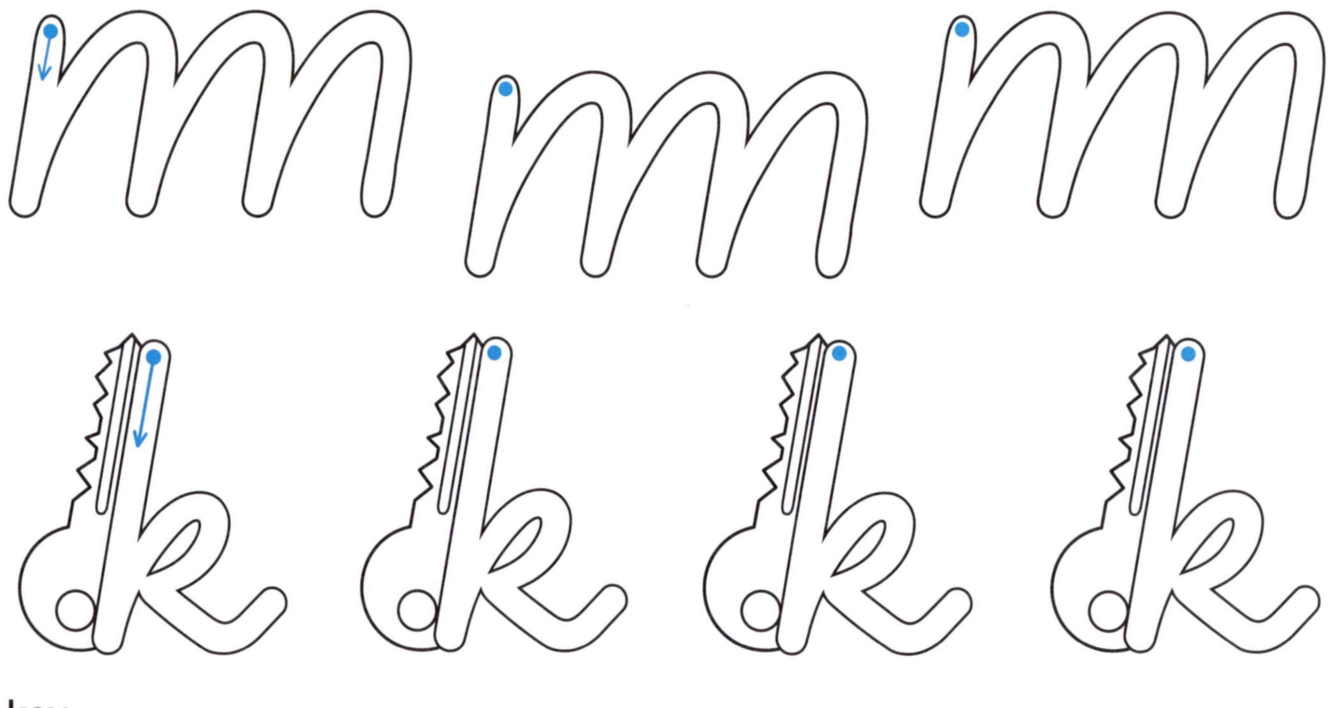

key

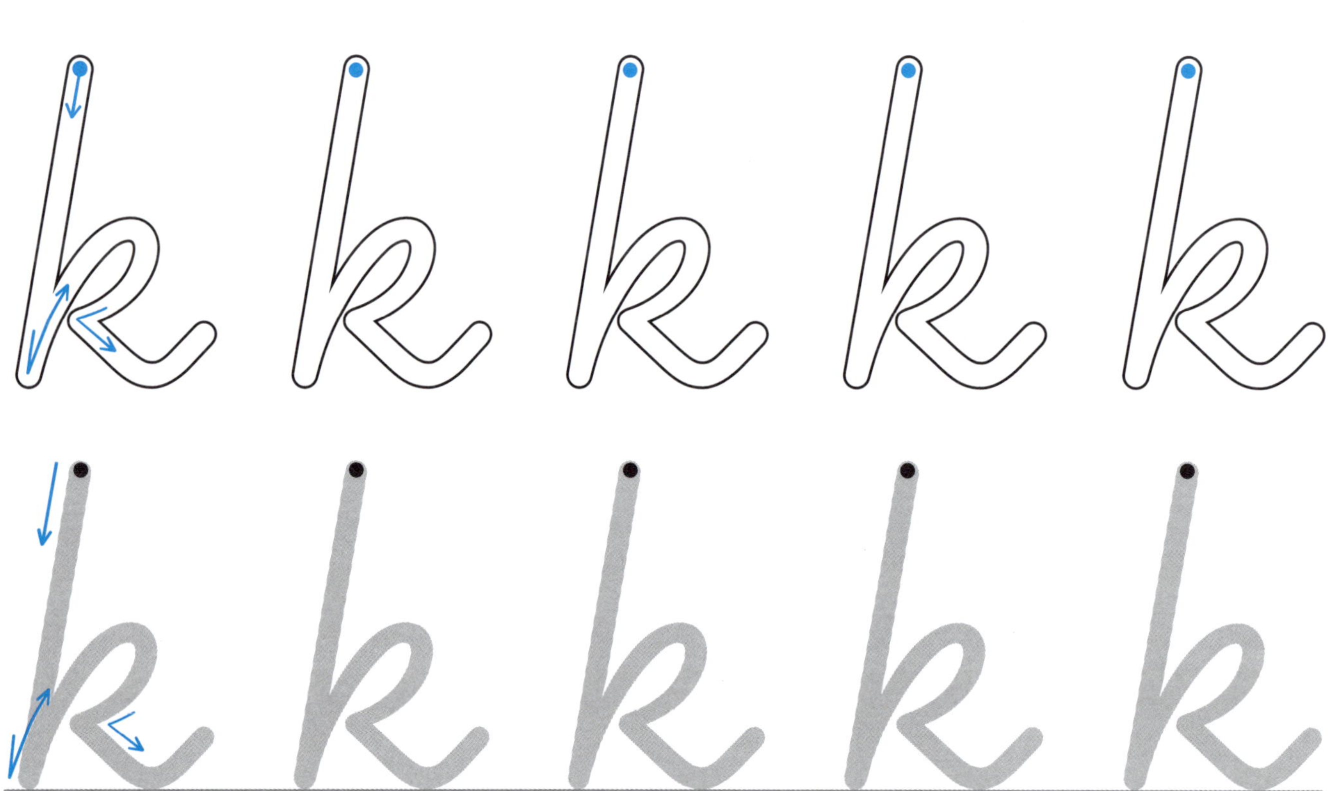

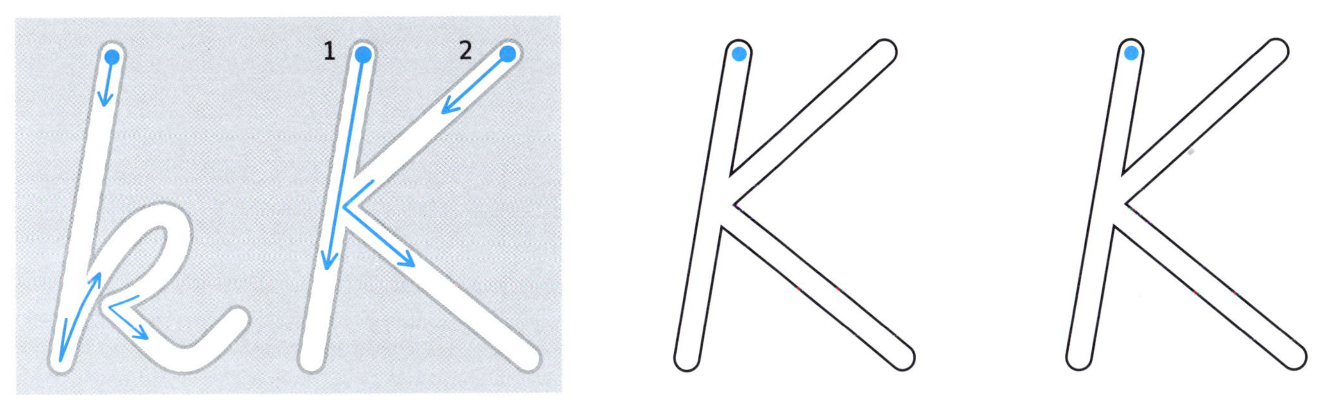

kangaroo

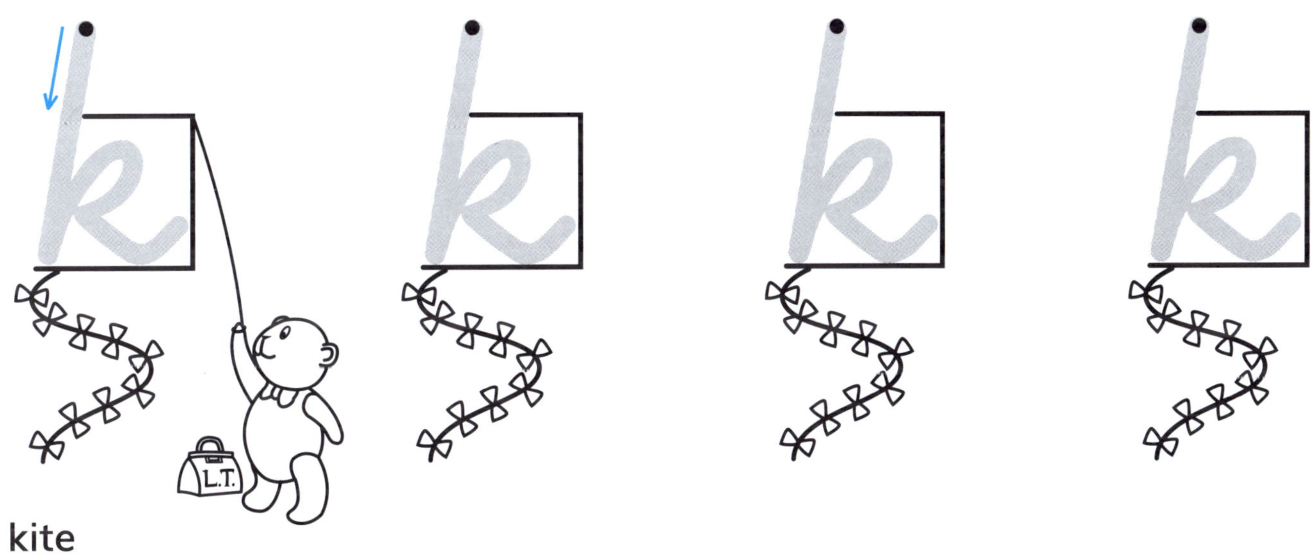

kite

Trace the letter.

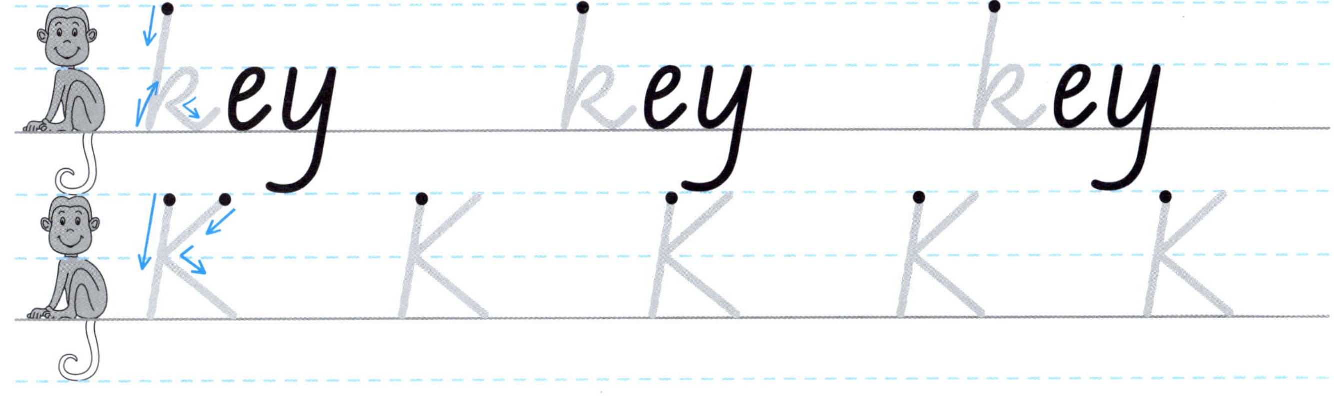

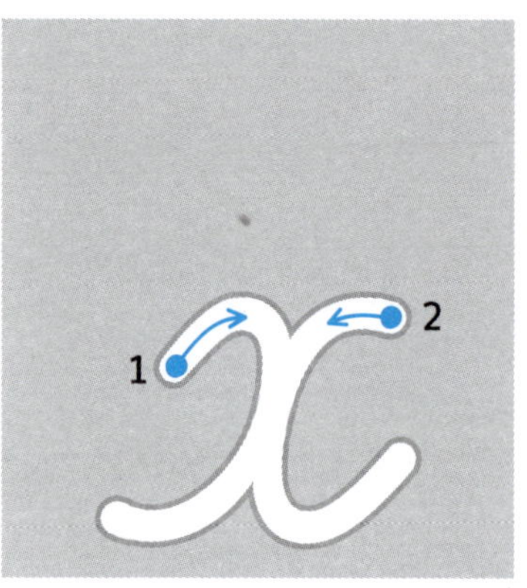

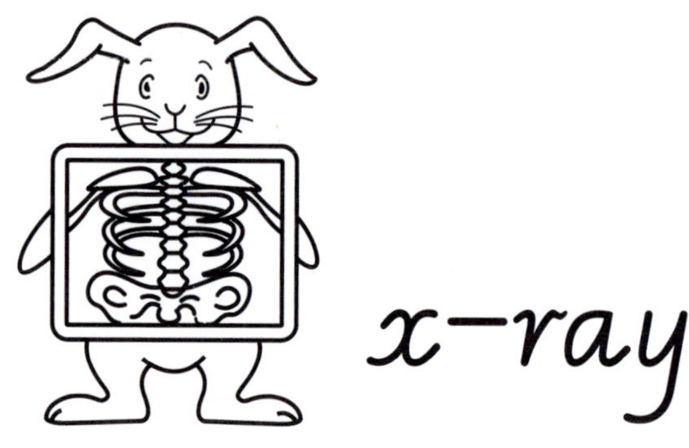

Start at the dot. Follow the arrow.

x-ray

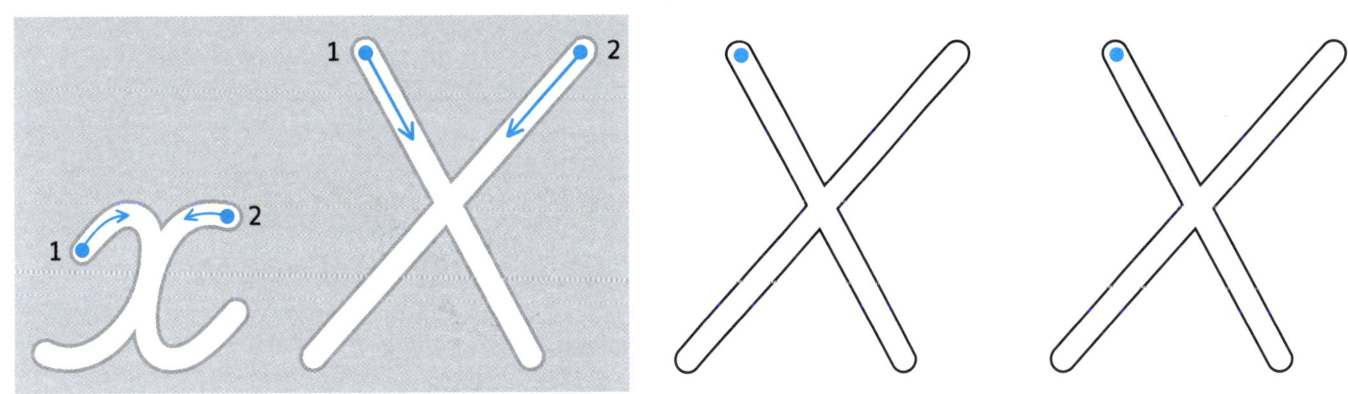

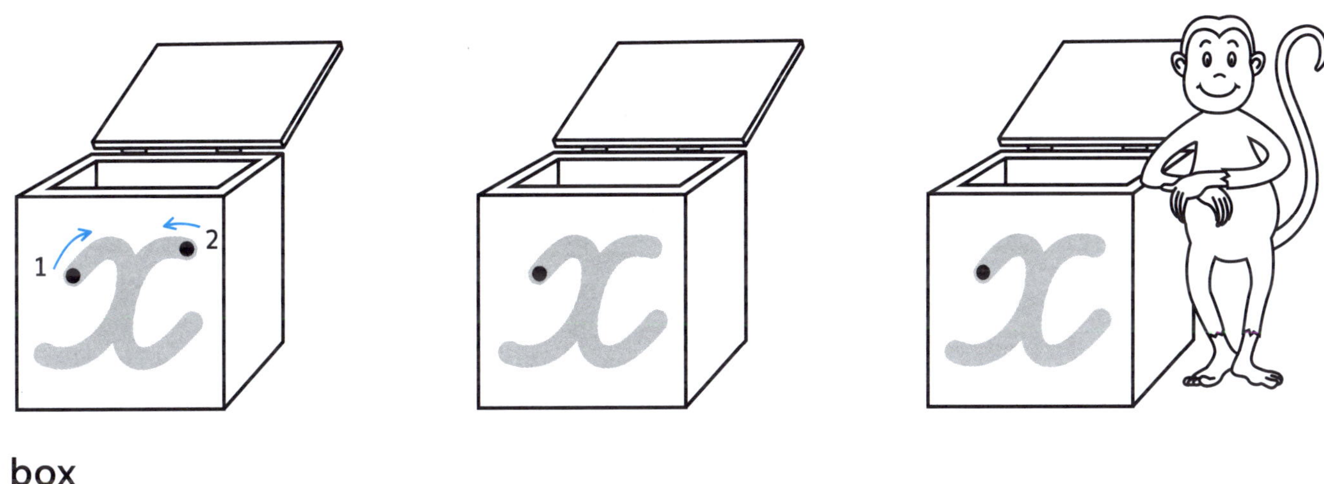

box

Trace the letter.

zoo

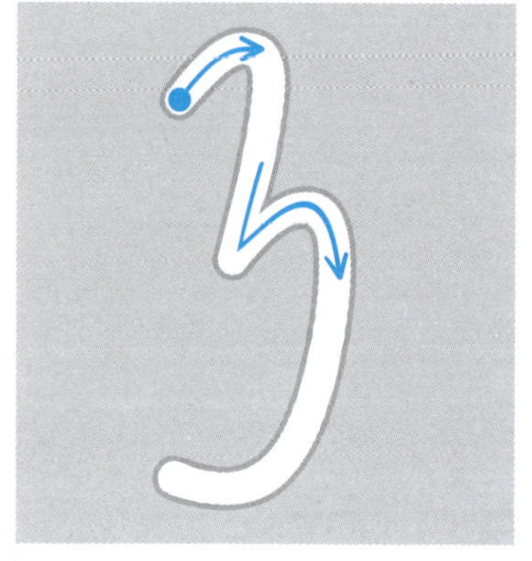

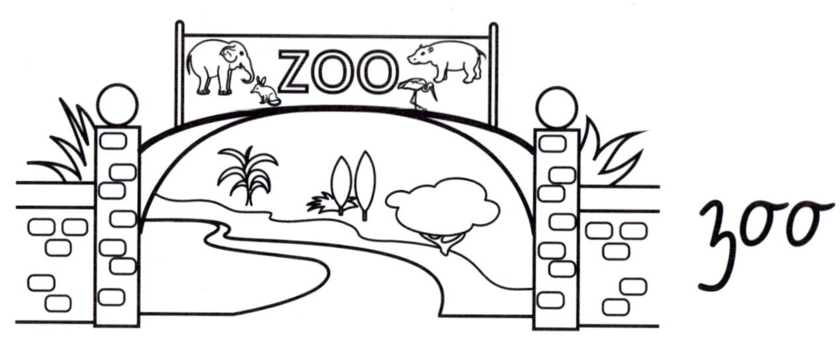

Start at the dot. Follow the arrow.

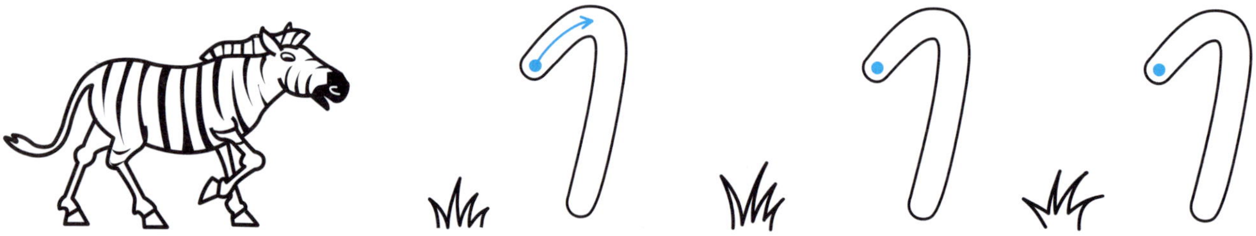

zebra

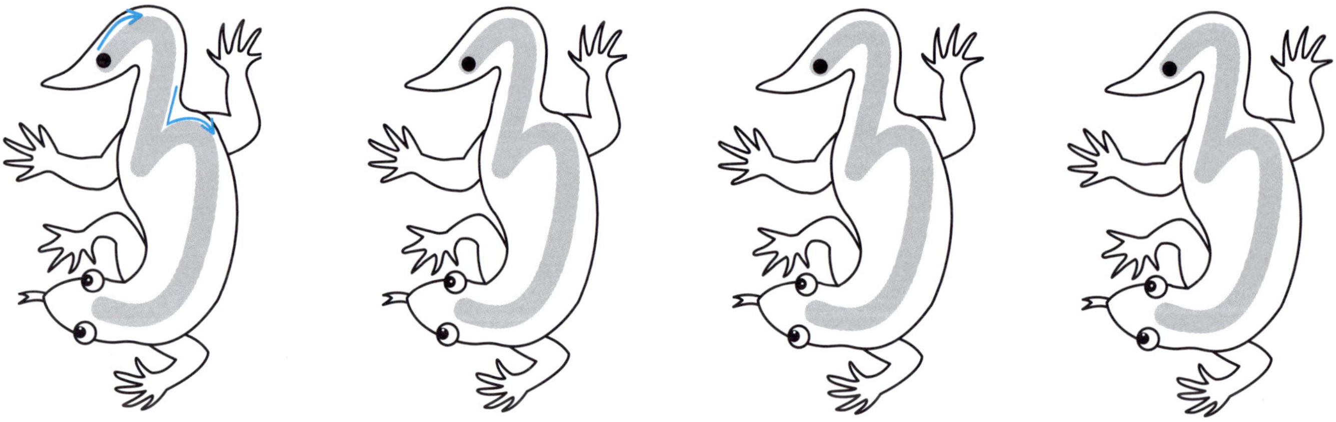

lizards

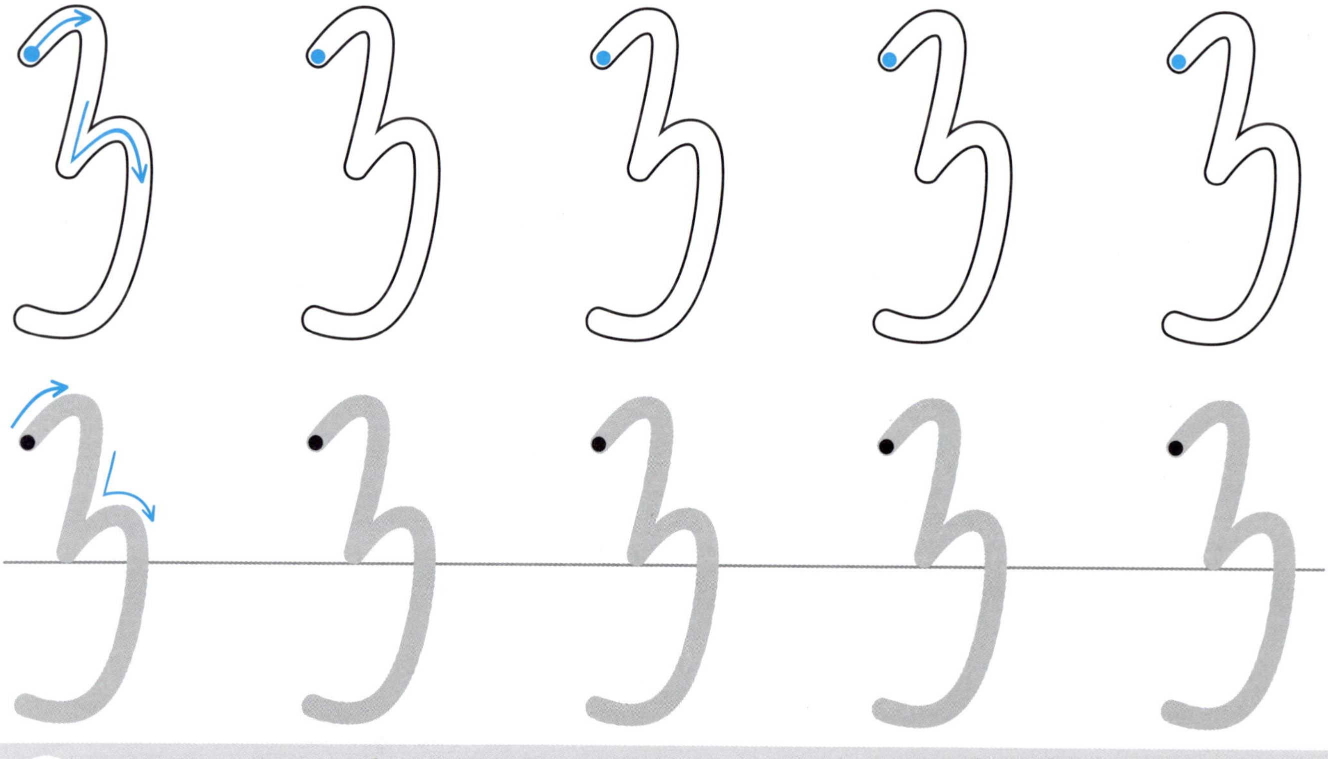

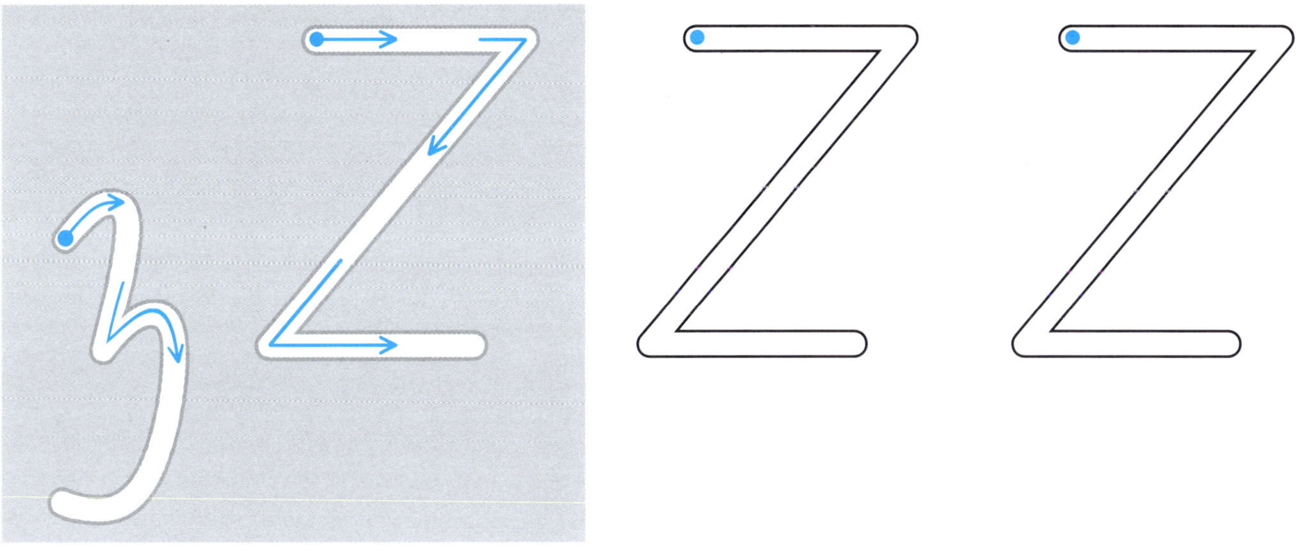

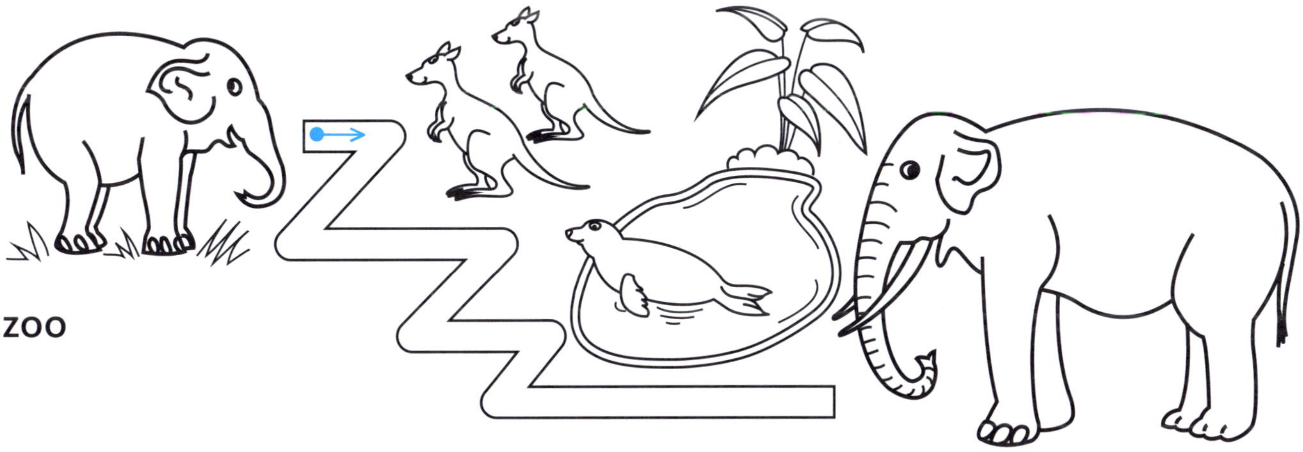

zoo

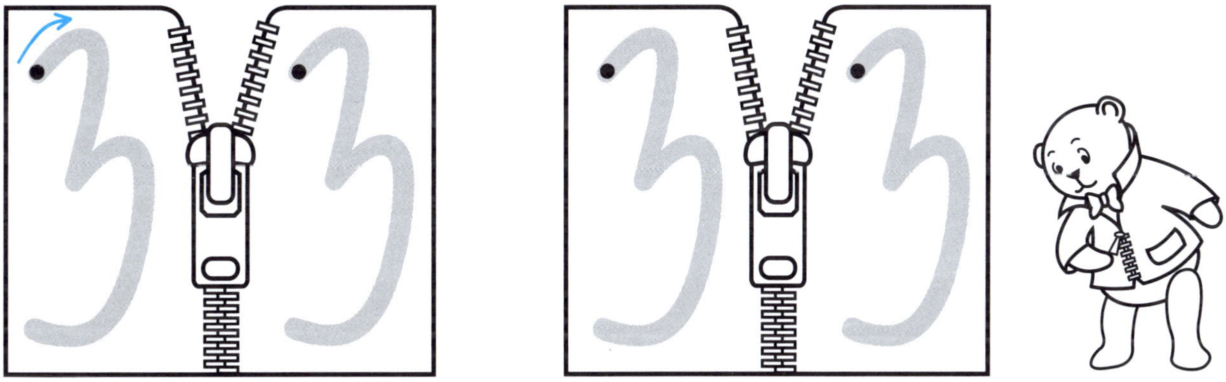

zip

Trace the letter.

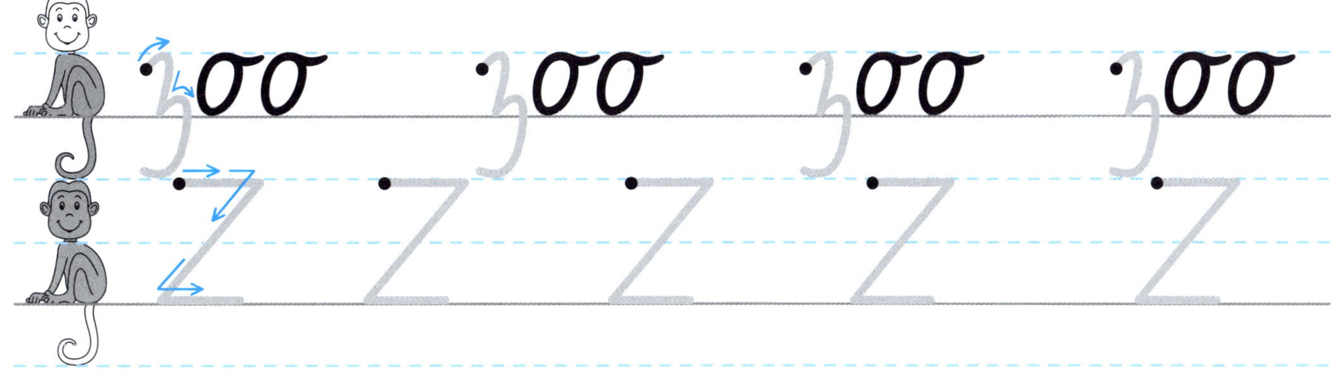

Trace and copy.

1 one

2 two

3 three

4 four

5 five

Trace and copy.

6 six

7 seven

8 eight

9 nine

10 ten

get.ga/PMWA206

Teacher observation guide

Student is: left-handed ☐ right-handed ☐

Student demonstrates correct posture, paper position and pencil grip. ☐

Student is stroking from top to bottom. ☐

Student is stroking from left to right. ☐

Student is tracking accurately using starting dots and arrows. ☐

Student is tracing accurately using starting dots and arrows. ☐

Student follows simple verbal rehearsals to form letters. ☐

Student forms lower-case letters of consistent size and with accuracy:

a	b	c	d	e	f	g	h	i	j	k	l	m	n	o	p	q	r	s	t	u	v	w	x	y	z

Student forms capital letters of consistent size and with accuracy:

A	B	C	D	E	F	G	H	I	J	K	L	M	N	O	P	Q	R	S	T	U	V	W	X	Y	Z

Student can write the numerals 1–10. ☐

Student uses head, body and tail character to describe the spatial properties of letters. ☐

Student has a growing ability to handwrite within lines. ☐

Notes:

....

....

....

....

Date: ....

CERTIFICATE

get.ga/PMWC200